Freedom
From Fear
Breaking free from Bondages

Kennedy R. Tajudeen

Kingdom Publishers

Freedom from Fear
Copyright©Kennedy Abdul-Rasak Tajudeen

All rights reserved. No part of this book may be reproduced in any form by photocopying or any electronic or mechanical means, including information storage or retrieval systems, without permission in writing from both the copyright owner and the publisher of the book. The right of Kennedy Abdul-Rasak Tajudeen to be identified as the author of this work has been asserted by him/her in accordance with the Copyright, Designs and Patents Act 1988 and any subsequent amendments thereto. A catalogue record for this book is available from the British Library.

ISBN: 978-1-913247-15-7

1st Edition by Kingdom Publishers
Kingdom Publishers, London, UK.

You can purchase copies of this book from any leading bookstore or email
contact@kingdompublishers.co.uk

Content

Dedication		7
Acknowledgement		9
Introduction		11
Chapter One:	Three Levels of Yirah	16
Chapter Two:	The Difference Between Fear of God and Devilish Fear	17
Chapter Three:	The Origin of Devilish Fear	25
Chapter Four:	Eleven Common Types of Fear	35
Chapter Five:	Entrance of Fear	56
Chapter Six:	Dangers of Living in Fear	62
Chapter Seven:	Fear Not	65
Chapter Eight:	Antidotes for Fear	67
Chapter Nine	The Power of Words	77

DEDICATION

I dedicate this moment to God the Father, God the Son and God the Holy Spirit. I acknowledge God my Father, Jesus Christ my Lord, Savior and Redeemer, the Holy Spirit, my Helper, Comforter and Advocate. I am who I am today because of God's grace and mercy upon my life. He is the One who saved me, raised me, healed me and restored me. I lift this book to God and dedicate it to Him, because there would have been no book if He had not breathed on me. So I thank God for this book and I bless the Holy Trinity for being that three corded rope in my life that can never be broken. To God only be all the glory. I also dedicate this book to all the women and men and I pray that you will be touched, healed and delivered from any fear in you. God richly bless you.

ACKNOWLEDGEMENT

First and foremost I would like to thank God. In the process of putting this book together I realised how true this gift of writing is for me. You given me the power to believe in my passion and pursue my dreams. I could never have done this without the faith I have in you, the Almighty.

INTRODUCTION

On January 19, 2010 while Ghana was enjoying her usual atmosphere of peace and tranquility, suddenly, there was a rumor of imminent earthquakes. Within a twinkle of an eye the news had spread around the streets, corners and communities of our nation. Everybody was engulfed with the fear of death, loss of goods and property. Nobody found comfort anymore in the comfort of their homes. Most Christians left their homes and resolved to live in their church premises to escape the devastation of the earthquakes. Those believers did not realize that safety and protection from the troubles of life is not in any church building but in Jesus Christ and in Him alone.

"1 He that dwelleth in the secret place of the Most High shall abide under the shadow of the Almighty. 2 I will say of the LORD, He is my refuge and my fortress: my God; in him will I trust. 3 Surely, he shall deliver thee from the snare of the fowler, and from the noisome pestilence. 4 He shall cover thee with his feathers, and under his wings shalt thou trust: his truth shall be thy shield and buckler. 5 Thou shalt not be afraid for the terror by night; nor for the arrow that flieth by day; 6 Nor for the pestilence that walketh in darkness; nor for the destruction that wasteth at noonday" (Psalms 91:1-6).

These verses of scripture clearly explain the truth about the PLACE of safety and protection. There is a place called the SECRET PLACE of the Most High God. In that secret place, God provides safety, deliverance, protection, and security for those who trust in HIM. That SECRET PLACE is Jesus Christ who is the embodiment of truth (Psalms 91:4). David said, "God's truth shall be his shield and buckler; that truth also represents God's word. His word, the Bible, is the only truth."

"6 Jesus saith unto him, I am the way, the truth, and the life: no man cometh unto the Father, but by me" (John 14:6).

Jesus openly declared in this verse that He is the truth and not a truth. "The" is a definite article – it means that Jesus is the definite and final truth; the truth that guarantees absolute security from the troubles of life. The Bible is loaded with the divine truth that pertains to life and godliness, but there is a problem with so many Christians in this dispensation. It is one thing to own a Bible and another thing to search out the truth in the Bible in order to acquire the knowledge of divine truth. . It is one thing to have Jesus Christ as your Lord and Savior and another thing to know Him. It takes a deeper relationship to know someone more closely, that is why it's required for Every Christian to walk with Jesus Christ in fellowship, prayer, fasting, and most essentially through His word.

"32 And ye shall know the truth, and the truth shall make you free" (John 8:32).

Having the truth is not the same as KNOWING the truth. For instance, if your father leaves you an inheritance unknown to you, probably the inheritance is worth millions of dollars; meanwhile you are going through financial difficulties which you could have easily handled if you had the knowledge of the inheritance that which was made available to you by your father – this means by right you are financially loaded but because you lack the knowledge of what you have by right, you are still wallowing in difficulties.

The first step to having access to the knowledge of the truth which is made available to you is to have the truth, but you are not supposed to stop there. You need to search out the truth which you have already possessed. There are people who are privileged to have good books (materials) in their hands but never make any effort in reading them which would have added value to their lives. Knowing the truth about Jesus living inside of you is what actually sets you free from the power of (the spirit of) fear and calamities of life. The truth itself does not set anyone free;, it's the knowledge of the truth that sets free.

KNOWLEDGE is the vehicle that gives you the access to exercise your right forto enjoying God's blessing.

The constitution of every nation provides the citizenry with vital information (knowledge) that will enable them to exercise their rights in order to enjoy the benefits of their nations. Most politicians have succeeded in manipulating people with the concept of democracy by presenting the rights of the people as if it is a privilege;, and the people accept such deception without arguing that it is manipulation of the highest degree, praising and applauding government for pretentiously giving them what belongs to them by right as if they are doing them an act of goodwill and favor. Lack of knowledge is the mystery behind such manipulations.

Many people have ended up in jail because they lack the knowledge of their constitutional rights as a bonafide citizen of their nations. Free education for some African countries is their constitutional right and not a favor done by politicians. Let me further explain this subject of "THE SECRET PLACE" with the story of Moses when he was desperately curious to see God's glory;, in other words, to see God.

"20 And he said, Thou canst not see my face: for there shall no man see me, and live" (Exodus 33:20).

God responded to Moses that such a request is out rightly impossible. The reason is simply to preserve Moses' life, so that he could continue with the assignment of leading the people to the Promised Land because nobody can see God and continue to live.

The devil also uses this statement in an opposing way to deceive his victims that nobody can see the troubles of life and still survive, but that statement has no basis for establishment in the life of the Christian because the Christian has been trained by the Holy Ghost to confront the storms of life with boldness. The righteous is as bold as a lion. We can work through the storms of life and emerge with victory. Praise God!!! Moses was a sincere seeker of God. So his request was granted upon an important condition – To every promise of God, there is a particular condition; all the promises of God are fulfilled and accessed in Christ Jesus. **For all the promises of God in him are yea, and in him Amen, unto the glory of God by us**. (2 **Corinthians** 1:**20**). ALL THE PROMISES OF GOD ARE ACCESIBLE , AND FULFILLED THROUGH JESUS CHRIST ALONE, NOT SOME OF THE PROMISES , BUT ALL. GLORY TO GOD!!!

The condition was that Moses would have to be kept in a particular place specifically in the cliff of a rock.

"21. And the LORD said, Behold, there is a place by me, and thou shalt stand upon a rock: 22 And it shall come to pass, while my glory passeth by, that I will put thee in a clift of the rock, and will cover thee with my hand while I pass by: 23 And I will take away mine hand, and thou shalt see my back parts: but my face shall not be seen" (Exodus 33:21-23).

That rock became a SECRET PLACE for Moses to be hidden so that when God passed by, Moses would not die. Those in Christ cannot die again because they have already died once with Christ. Consequently, they are born again to live again and this time, to live forever in eternity with God – Hallelujah!!!

There is a place where you are hidden permanently where no disaster can catch up with you; that secret place is JESUS CHRIST (1 Corinthians 10:4). ***"4 And did all drink the same spiritual drink: for they drank of that spiritual Rock that followed them: and that Rock was Christ."***

Those who confessed Christ as their savior during the earthquake hoax soon denounced Him when the rumored date was past. Initially, they were afraid of spending eternity in hell fire after death but soon after, they went back to their old lives. True repentance cannot be measured through the fear of hell or death. The love of God should always be the motivation for genuine repentance. Salvation that is founded and established on the love of God will always survive the test of time.

Those who confess Jesus Christ out of fear of hell and death will soon give up on God when the mirage of fear disappears. The former prime minister of the United Kingdom, **Tony Blair**, once said in an interview that those who claim to love God due to the fear of hell do not really love Him as they claim. The most significant reason for loving God should be centered on the fact that He is our Creator and that He first loved us; so we have no option than to love Him in return.

Loving God should not be an opportunity to escape His judgment of eternal doom, but because He is God and He deserves to be feared. This fear is not a terrible fear but fear out of respect and honor. In this book, we will explore great mysteries which will bring an utter end to any kind of devilish fear operating in your life. I encourage you to read this book prayerfully and your life will never be the same again. May the Lord empower you to walk in the dimension of God's kind of fear in Jesus' mighty name, Amen.

WHAT IS FEAR?

Fear is a feeling induced by perceived danger or threat. This occurs in certain types of organs which causes changes in metabolism and organ functions and ultimately a change in behavior such as fleeing, hiding, worry, anxiety, and freezing without being able to make any positive movement in life because of perceived traumatic events.

Fear is an unpleasant emotion or thought when you are frightened or worried about something dangerous, painful, or bad that is happening to you or might happen to you. The word fear is from the Greek word *'phobos'* meaning fear, and that is where the English word **PHOBIA** (an extreme fear of a particular animal, place, situation or people) was derived from – *'Phobos'* means panic, fright, terror, fear.

The Hebrew word for fear is *'Yirah'* which has diverse meaning in scripture — sometimes, it refers to the fear we feel in anticipation of some danger or pain, but it can also mean reverence or awe. *Yirah,* when it refers to God's reverence, also includes an overwhelming sense of the glory, worth, beauty, amazement, mystery, astonishment, gratitude and even worship of the One True God.

CHAPTER ONE

THREE LEVELS OF YIRAH

1. The first level is the fear of unpleasant consequences or punishment and that is pronounced as **"Yirat hanesh"** – This type of fear prevents people from doing the wrong thing in order to avoid punishment or consequences for their actions. Crime would become the norm in society if there was no FEAR of being punished by the law. It is the kind of fear that operates in people so that they could avoid public disgrace and ridicule. This is the reason many people are comfortable doing the wrong things when no one is watching because they lack the consciousness of the omnipresence of God.

2. The second level of fear concerns anxiety over breaking God's Law — sSometimes it is called *Yirat hamalkhut*. This is the foundation of the concept of karma (the law of Karma). This kind of fear propels people to do good so that they can avoid being punished or retributed either by God or by the law of nature (natural law) in this life, or in the world to come. The motive behind those who practice such acts of fear is always mixed; it is either a genuine desire to honor God or an opportunity to avoid God's righteous wrath against sin.

3. The third level of fear is the highest kind which is a profound reverence for God. This level of fear discerns the presence of God in all things. Sometimes it is called *Yirat harommemnut*. Through this fear we behold the glory of God and His majesty in all things.

    To reverence means to show a deep and solemn respect. It is our attitude of deep respect with awe; it is an emotion through recognition and acknowledgement of God.

CHAPTER TWO

DIFFERENCE BETWEEN THE FEAR OF GOD AND DEVILISH

The simple and fundamental meaning of the FEAR OF GOD is to depart from evil.

"6 By mercy and truth iniquity is purged: and by the fear of the LORD men depart from evil." (Proverbs 16:6).

To depart means to part ways with something that is originally part of you. But the fear of the devil comes with an enticement to perpetually attach us to evil, worry, desperation, anxiety, doubt, and hopelessness.

"The fear of the LORD is the beginning of wisdom: and the knowledge of the holy is understanding" (Proverbs 9:10). .In this verse, we saw three key words which plays significant role in the subject of the fear of God : 1. KNOWLEDGE 2. WISDOM. 3. UNDERSTANDING. KNOWLEDGE is the acquisition of information, (information could either be right or wrong) glory to God the Bible is the right information from God. UNDERSTANDING is the ability to analyse the right information, and arrive at the right point. WISDOM is the right application of the right analysed information you acquired. Wrong information will always produce wrong understanding , and anything you understood wrongly would be wrongly applied. Sometimes you might have the right information, but if the information is wrongly understood, misapplication is inevitable. That is why you come across certain people who have knowledge about the Bible, yet they argue the truth of God's word with passion, the reason is because they lacked the vital aspect of the deal which is UNDERSTANDING. No matter how much you learn or study, if you don't understand what you have learnt, you will definitely misapply it. **Mathew.13:23 But he that received seed into the good ground is he that heareth the word, and understandeth it; which also beareth fruit, and bringeth forth, some an hundredfold, some sixty, some thirty.** In the parable of sower which Jesus used to illustrate how the word of God functions , you will realize that the difference between those who were fruitful and those who are not is simply UNDERSTANDING. Though all of them received the

word, but those who understood it brought forth thirty, sixty and hundred dimension of harvests. They rightly applied the word and it brought forth a great profit to them.

The Bible says the fear of the Lord is the beginning of WISDOM, but not wisdom in it's totality ; it is just the beginning of WISDOM. Now, if the fear of God is just the beginning of wisdom, it means that wisdom begins from somewhere — the beginning of wisdom starts from the moment you confess Jesus Christ as your Lord and Savior and we are expected to walk in this wisdom until we end our journey on this earth.

What is wisdom? Wisdom is the right application of the right and true information from God. That information is the knowledge of God's Word which is the true light. The entrance of God's Word gives light and understanding to the simple.

"130 The entrance of thy words giveth light; it giveth understanding unto the simple" (Psalm 119:130).

The word knowledge here is the Light that has the capacity to dispel every form of darkness — darkness represents ignorance., and sin.

"6 My people are destroyed for lack of knowledge: because thou hast rejected knowledge, I will also reject thee, that thou shalt be no priest to me: seeing thou hast forgotten the law of thy God, I will also forget thy children" (Hosea 4:6).

The Bible says people are destroyed or perished for lack of knowledge and not lack of wisdom. Why not lack of wisdom? The reason is because without KNOWLEDGE (LIGHT), there cannot be WISDOM — wisdom is the right application of knowledge. You can't practice what you don't have knowledge about. God expects us to travel with wisdom on daily basis to ensure our daily victory over Satan and his demonic strategies.

"13 Let us hear the conclusion of the whole matter: Fear God, and keep his commandments: for this is the whole duty of man" (Ecclesiastes 12:13).

King Solomon was one of the most powerful kings in Israel who was endowed with divine wisdom to govern Israel. Solomon received an impartation of divine wisdom the night that he had an encounter with God through a dream just as anyone who has an encounter with God through the acceptance of Jesus Christ receives divine wisdom. Along the line, however, Solomon stopped functioning in the order of divine wisdom. He allowed the enticement of strange women to capture his heart, and eventually, he began to worship strange gods introduced to him by these strange women. He later repented after realizing that the way of foolishness is an easy entrance to hell and destruction. He was inspired by God to write the book of Ecclesiastes after he repented from backsliding. In the book of Ecclesiastes, God used him to address so many issues that admonish us to be dedicated to godly living. He also stressed on the necessity of constantly living in holiness for every Christian (believer).

In his concluding chapter of Ecclesiastes, he made a profound statement that we should all give our utmost attention and be ready to practice if we truly desire to live eternally with God in heaven. (Ecclesiastes 12:13). The verse of the scripture explained how the fear of God works – Solomon says, **"FEAR GOD AND OBEY HIS COMMANDMENT"** – this simply means without the fear of God, it is impossible to obey God. Our commitment to obeying God in the closet enforces and triggers reward and promotion in God's Kingdom.

"4 That thine alms may be in secret: and thy Father which seeth in secret himself shall reward thee openly" (Matthew 6:4).

The fear of God refers to awe, honor, and respect for Him. It is this kind of fear that enables us to obey God without compulsion – this kind of fear does not portray God as a scary and horrible entity, but it is the fear that instills the respect and honor for God, so that we don't compromise His Word in the face of a tempting situation. Brother Joseph was an uncompromising personality who exhibited the fear of God in the face of a tempting situation (Genesis 39:5-20).

It is obviously easy to refuse and never bow to temptation in the open where everyone is watching, but the true act of rebellion against temptation is mostly accepted and rewarded by God when it is practiced in secret, especially where no one is watching. Satan is full of evil schemes; he mostly presents sin to us in secret where no one is watching so that sin will be registered against us. We will eventually be demoted instead of being promoted in the spirit and in the physical when we yield to sin – we experience promotion, blessings, and fulfillment of God's promises whenever we refuse to bow to temptations – but we experience the opposite whenever we bow to Satan and his schemes. A lot of Christians experience retrogression and demotion because we bow to sSatanic schemes in secret even though no one sees us, but we lose so much from God, the giver of good blessings.

"11 And it came to pass about this time, that Joseph went into the house to do his business; and there was none of the men of the house there within" (Genesis 39:11).

Interestingly, the temptation of Joseph took place in the closet where no one was available, yet he refused to yield to the temptation sharply why? The answer to this question is packaged in Genesis 39:9.

"9 There is none greater in this house than I; neither hath he kept back anything from me but thee, because thou art his wife: how then can I do this great wickedness, and sin against God?"

Joseph made a profound statement by saying: How can I do this great wickedness and sin against God? He considered sinning against his master as equal to sinning against God. Though nobody was present when Joseph was being tempted, yet he was extremely conscious of the Omnipresent God — He had a great reverential FEAR (respect) for God; so he could not sin against the invisible God before whom all things are naked.

Joseph's decision to fear God (respect and honor God) entrapped him to be falsely accused and he eventually landed in prison, but God later rewarded his faithfulness by elevating him to the highest office in Egypt, a foreign land.

"41 And Pharaoh said unto Joseph, See, I have set thee over all the land of Egypt. 42 And Pharaoh took off his ring from his hand, and put it upon Joseph's hand, and arrayed him in vestures of fine linen, and put a gold chain about his neck; 43 And he made him to ride in the second chariot which he had; and they cried before him, Bow the knee: and he made him ruler over all the land of Egypt" (Genesis 41:41-43).

It is naturally impossible for any responsible child to misbehave in the presence of a respectable parent, but the only time this can be possible is if the parents are irresponsible. For instance, if a father is addicted to smoking, the child may also consider smoking as a normal act which will attract no questioning from the father. But if the father is responsible, no child in his or her right frame of mind would ever do such a thing. God is holy and that is His standard; sSo anyone who accepts God as his or her father must live up to God's standard.

The fear of God, a deep and solemn respect for God, will disallow you from disrespecting and misbehaving before Him. God is not only a holy God but He is also an Omnipresent God, and whatever we do in the secret is naked before Him.

"7 Whither shall I go from thy spirit? Oor whither shall I flee from thy presence? 8 If I ascend up into heaven, thou art there: if I make my bed in hell, behold, thou art there. 9 If I take the wings of the morning, and dwell in the uttermost parts of the sea; 10 Even there shall thy hand lead me, and thy right hand shall hold me. 11 If I say, Surely the darkness shall cover me; even the night shall be light about me. 12 Yea, the darkness hideth not from thee; but the night shineth as the day: the darkness and the light are both alike to thee" (Psalm 139:7-12).

Thus, it is required of us to reverence God in every area of our lives. The fear of life's situations and circumstances is always programmed by the devil to gain access into our minds, and the secret agenda is to compel or entice us to compromise our duty and responsibility to respect and honor God, our father. The trial of Shadrach, Meshach and Abednego manifested in two ways and within different environments.

1. Test and Trial.

    "3 Knowing this, that the trying of your faith worketh patience" (James 1:3).

2. Temptation.

    "13 Let no man say when he is tempted, I am tempted of God: for God cannot be tempted with evil, neither tempteth he any man" (James 1:13).

Trial or test is a platform for examination where God tests our faith to prepare us for the next level of blessings and promotion. God cannot entrust bigger assignments into our hands if He has not tested our faith. Just as no student is qualified to gain entrance to the next class or level in academic pursuit without writing an examination. It is the score in the examination that will determine whether the student would be promoted, or repeat the class. "FAITH THAT IS NOT TESTED CANNOT BE TRUSTED".

"12 And he said, Lay not thine hand upon the lad, neither do thou anything unto him: for now I know that thou fearest God, seeing thou hast not withheld thy son, thine only son from me. 13 And Abraham lifted up his eyes, and looked, and behold behind him a ram caught in a thicket by his horns: and Abraham went and took the ram, and offered him up for a burnt offering in the stead of his son. 14 And Abraham called the name of that place Jehovahjireh: as it is said to this day, In the mount of the LORD it shall be seen. 15 And the angel of the LORD called unto Abraham out of

heaven the second time, 16 And said, By myself have I sworn, saith the LORD, for because thou hast done this thing, and hast not withheld thy son, thine only son: 17 That in blessing I will bless thee, and in multiplying I will multiply thy seed as the stars of the heaven, and as the sand which is upon the sea shore; and thy seed shall possess the gate of his enemies; 18 And in thy seed shall all the nations of the earth be blessed; because thou hast obeyed my voice. 19 So Abraham returned unto his young men, and they rose up and went together to Beersheba; and Abraham dwelt at Beersheba" (Genesis 22:12-19).

At this point in Abraham's life, he had walked with God for several years and he was one hundred years old but God never trusted him with greater blessing,s and multiplication until he passed the examination of sacrificing Isaac, his only son with promise. He sacrificed Isaac not because he was afraid of being punished by God, but because he had great respect for God. True obedience emanates from genuine respect and not from fear of punishment (Genesis 22:12).

Temptation is a demonic enticement placed upon our flesh to desire evil in order to disobey God. Desiring good things is not evil but what we do to fulfill the desire, and how we go about fulfilling the desire would either make it good or evil. **Timothy 3:1 This is a true saying, if a man desire the office of a bishop, he desireth a good work. 3:2 A bishop then must be blameless, the husband of one wife, vigilant, sober, of good behaviour, given to hospitality, apt to teach;3:3 Not given to wine, no striker, not greedy of filthy lucre; but patient, not a brawler, not covetous;3:4 One that ruleth well his own house, having his children in subjection with all gravity;3:5 (For if a man know not how to rule his own house, how shall he take care of the church of God?)3:6 Not a novice, lest being lifted up with pride he fall into the condemnation of the devil.3:7 Moreover, he must have a good report of them which are without; lest he fall into reproach and the snare of the devil.3:8 Likewise must the deacons be grave, not double-tongued, not given to much wine, not greedy of filthy lucre;3:9 Holding the mystery of the faith in a pure conscience)** we see clearly in this verses of the scriptures that Apostle Paul was not only addressing the issue of desiring the office of a Bishop, which is obviously a good desire, but he went further to stressed on the necessity of what to do, and how to birth that good desire into fulfilment. For instance, if you desire to have sex, it's a good desire, but that desire must be fulfilled within the confine of marriage between a man and a woman. If you desire to own a good car, mansion, it's a good desire but that desire would be considered evil, if you fulfill those desires through diabolical means . Temptation itself is not a sin because everyone is tempted (James 1:14), but falling into the temptation makes it a sin; even Jesus was tempted by the devil, but He did not sin. **Hebrews 4:15 For we have not an high priest which cannot be touched with the feeling of our infirmities; but was in all points tempted like as we are, yet without sin.** (Matthew 4:1). Everyone living under the heavens is tempted on a daily basis, but a Christian is trained and admonished by God not to yield to temptation.

Temptations and trials operate in parallel anytime a Christian is confronted with challenges. Whenever we are being tempted by Satan, God also tests us. Temptation comes to entice us to disobey God in order to rob us of our blessing and promotion while at the same time God tests our faith whether we will obey Him, so that He can bless and promote us. God does not tempt anyone (James 1:13). The temptation of Shadrack, Meshack and Abednego occurred in two different environments: (1) In the open among the crowd (2) In the secret before King Nebuchadnezzar.

"1 Nebuchadnezzar the king made an image of gold, whose height was threescore cubits, and the breadth thereof six cubits: he set it up in the plain of Dura, in the province of Babylon. 2 Then Nebuchadnezzar the king sent to gather together the princes, the governors, and the captains, the judges, the treasurers, the counsellors, the sheriffs, and all the rulers of the provinces, to come to the dedication of the image which Nebuchadnezzar the king had set up. 3 Then the princes, the governors, and captains, the judges, the treasurers, the counsellors, the sheriffs, and all the rulers of the provinces, were gathered together unto the dedication of the image that Nebuchadnezzar the king had set up; and they stood before the image that Nebuchadnezzar had set up. 4 Then an herald cried aloud, To you it is commanded, O people, nations, and languages, 5 That at what time ye hear the sound of the cornet, flute, harp, sackbut, psaltery, dulcimer, and all kinds of music, ye fall down and worship the golden image that Nebuchadnezzar the king hath set up: 6 And whoso falleth not down and worshippeth shall the same hour be cast into the midst of a burning fiery furnace. 7 Therefore at that time, when all the people heard the sound of the cornet, flute, harp, sackbut, psaltery, and all kinds of music, all the people, the nations, and the languages, fell down and worshipped the golden image that Nebuchadnezzar the king had set up" (Daniel 3:1-7).

This temptation and test occurred in an open place where everyone in the province of Babylon was commanded by the king to gather in order to bow to the golden image that he had erected. But these three uncompromising Jews refused to bow in the open. In Daniel 3:12-13,

"12 There are certain Jews whom thou hast set over the affairs of the province of Babylon, Shadrach, Meshach, and Abednego; these men, O king, have not regarded thee: they serve not thy gods, nor worship the golden image which thou hast set up. 13 Then Nebuchadnezzar in his rage and fury commanded to bring Shadrach, Meshach, and Abednego. Then they brought these men before the king."

This test and temptation also occurred at a different place. At this point they had been taken out of the crowd as commanded by the king in his fury. They were in an environment where it would have been easy for them to compromise their faith in the true and living God. They were in the secret before the earthly king where no other Israelite who knew about the depth of this commandment of God were present (thou shall not bow to any image (Exodus 20: 5-6). The devil is very organized in arranging a secret place to present temptation to us where no one will discover that we have already compromised our faith in God. Though these three Jews stood before the powerful earthly king who has already decreed that whosoever will disobey his commandment will suffer the punishment of heated fire, yet they decided to obey the commandment of the invisible God who sees and knows all things.

"5 Thou shalt not bow down thyself to them, nor serve them: for I the LORD thy God am a jealous God, visiting the iniquity of the fathers upon the children unto the third and fourth generation of them that hate me" (Exodus 20:5).

They offered to God His due respect (reverenced fear) by obeying His commandment and that uncompromising decision led to their unhindered promotion and blessing (Daniel 3:29-30).

Our obedience and respect for God in the secret enforces and triggers open reward and promotion and not just what we do for people to see. God is a Spirit who sees all things in the spirit and in the physical. He mostly deals with us in our secret places and rewards us openly (Matthew 6:4).

CHAPTER THREE

THE ORIGIN OF DEVILISH FEAR

"9 And the LORD God called unto Adam, and said unto him, Where art thou? 10 And he said, I heard thy voice in the garden, and I was afraid, because I was naked; and I hid myself. 11 And he said, Who told thee that thou wast naked? Hast thou eaten of the tree, whereof I commanded thee that thou shouldest not eat?"

(Genesis 3:9-11)

In life, every situation that affects humanity, either positively or negatively, emanates from a source. To every situation or problem, there is always a solution, but the problem with many of us is that we take delight in searching for solution without tracing the source of the situation from its root in order to ensure a permanent solution — If a tree is cut from the middle, it will still grow and germinate if the roots are still deeply rooted in the soil. Similarly, any situation that is not particularly dealt with from the root will not be permanently solved unless we discover the origin. This is the reason why some people experience joy and happiness for a moment and within a short space of time that atmosphere of happiness disappears suddenly, simply because their fear has surfaced again . It is because they have not made the effort in discovering the source of that reoccurring circumstance.

Similarly, demonic fear has a source but if we don't trace its root from source, we will remain permanent slaves to fear. Now, carefully follow me through the leading of the Holy Spirit to expose the source of this deadly sSatanic agent called fear. The word fear was first mentioned in Genesis 3:10; *"I was afraid"*. The phrase "I was afraid" was said for the first time by Adam. The question is: why was Adam afraid? He heard aA" voice" in the garden and he was afraid. The answer is because he heard a VOICE. What is a VOICE? It is a sound that is uttered by any living being to call for attention. The Bible talks about different kinds of voices in this world.

"10 There are, it may be, so many kinds of voices in the world, and none of them is without signification" (1 Corinthian 14:10).

All these voices have significance; in other words, they all have different meanings and effects.

Three kinds of voices from Greek rendering:

1. Foni   : Speech, Cry, Call
2. Lalia   : Speech
3. Ekfrazo : Express, Enunciate

All these three meanings are still tilted towards calling or crying to get one's attention. The voice of God through His Word is the most powerful and significant VOICE.

"12 For the word of God is quick, and powerful, and sharper than any two-edged sword, piercing even to the dividing asunder of soul and spirit, and of the joints and marrow, and is a discerner of the thoughts and intents of the heart" (Hebrews 4:12).

God's VOICE always travels with an assignment to call the attention of sinners to repentance; the attention of the foolish to sound wisdom; the attention of the poor to the true and great riches and blessing in Christ; evil deeds to good deeds; and broad way to the narrow gate. Any voice which does not promote the principles and doctrines of Jesus Christ is a demonic voice which leads to death and destruction. Be careful of the voices you listen to!!! Be careful of the voices of wrong friends!!!

In Genesis 3:1-5, we read, *"1 Now the serpent was more subtle than any beast of the field which the LORD God had made. And he said unto the woman, Yea, hath God said, Ye shall not eat of every tree of the garden? 2 And the woman said unto the serpent, We may eat of the fruit of the trees of the garden: 3 But of the fruit of the tree which is in the midst of the garden, God hath said, Ye shall not eat of it, neither shall ye touch it, lest ye die. 4 And the serpent said unto the woman, Ye shall not surely die: 5 For God doth know that in the day ye eat thereof, then your eyes shall be opened, and ye shall be as gods, knowing good and evil"*, there was an expression of a particular VOICE calling for Eve's attention to disobey God's Laws, and command, and Eve also transferred that voice to her husband, Adam. Thereby, sSatanic fear was introduced and took immediate effect in the spirit the moment Adam and Eve disobeyed God by obeying Satan's VOICE of deceit. — VOICE – DECEIT- DISOBEDIENCE. Fear is always traceable to VOICE, DECEIT and DISOBEDIENCE. Fear was borne out of lies and that is why we have the acronym below:

F – **F**ALSE
E – **E**VIDENCE
A – **A**PPEARING
R – **R**EAL

Whereas faith is:

F – **F**ACTS
A – **A**CCEPTED
I – **I**N
T – **T**HE
H – **H**EART

FOUR CULPRITS

There were four culprits who played a heinous role in the incident that led to the fall of man – these four culprits stood before the Supreme Court judge of heaven. The God of heaven who is a righteous judge sat on the case. The four culprits were: (1) Adam (2) Eve (3) Serpent (4) Satan. In judicial matters, no judge has the right to sentence an accused person without finding him or her guilty – it is also a necessity in legal matters that the accused person or his or her lawyer (representative) should be given the right to speak in his or her defense before the judge could pass a verdict.

God questioned Adam who was given the right to speak in his defense. Eve was also given the opportunity to speak. They were both found guilty and sentence was passed on them (Genesis 3:16-18).

"16 Unto the woman he said, I will greatly multiply thy sorrow and thy conception; in sorrow thou shalt bring forth children; and thy desire shall be to thy husband, and he shall rule over thee. 17 And unto Adam he said, Because thou hast hearkened unto the voice of thy wife, and hast eaten of the tree, of which I commanded thee, saying, Thou shalt not eat of it: cursed is the ground for thy sake; in sorrow shalt thou eat of it all the days of thy life."

The serpent was just a natural animal like any other animal that God created but it was more subtle than any other animal which the Lord had made. Eve was comfortable dialoging with the serpent from the beginning, and she felt no sense of fear. Fear was introduced the moment they disobeyed God and the same animal that was so friendly to them suddenly became a fearful creature to them.

"1 Now the serpent was more subtle than any beast of the field which the LORD God had made. And he said unto the woman, Yea, hath God said, Ye shall not eat of every tree of the garden?" (Genesis 3:1).

In his defense, Adam said it was the woman (Genesis 3:12): *"12 And the man said, The woman whom thou gavest to be with me, she gave me of the tree, and I did eat."* Eve, in her defense, also pushed the blame to the serpent by saying: "The Serpent beguiled me;" in other words, deceived me, (Genesis 3:13): *"13 And the LORD God said unto the woman, What is this that thou hast done? And the woman said, The serpent beguiled me, and I did eat."*

At that point, Satan had already left the serpent after using it as an agent of temptation against man. Naturally, serpents don't speak; they only hiss but Satan used the subtlety of the serpent to speak to Eve deceptively. Eve probably fell into that satanic deception because she realized that the serpent was dumb right from creation, but had started speaking all of a sudden. Eve, in her amazement, would begin to reason in her mind – "What is happening here?" In her curiosity, she might finally conclude that the deception of Satan about them being like God could be true if they should eat the forbidden fruit. She must have been convinced enough that the serpent had also taken a bite of the tree of the knowledge of good and evil; thus, the change she saw.

In the Bible, a serpent is a symbolic description of Satan because it is subtle and cunning in nature. Satan's decision to use a serpent as an agent of temptation against man was because he needed a vessel that possessed such a subtle and cunning character in order to achieve his deceptive agenda. If you are handsome and clever, he can easily use you to deceive women to their hurts, he does likewise to men by using the beauty of women to deceive them to destruction. May you not become an agent in the hands the devil in Jesus name Amen That is why I can safely say that Satan can hardly tempt you with what you don't like or need. He is an expert in using our weaknesses to tempt us. He will not use a beautiful lady to tempt a man who does not have sexual desire for woman.

"22 Then Peter took him, and began to rebuke him, saying, Be it far from thee, Lord: this shall not be unto thee. 23 But he turned, and said unto Peter, Get thee behind me, Satan: thou art an offence unto me: for thou savourest not the things that be of God, but those that be of men." (Matthew 16:22-23).

Jesus was just at the climax of fulfilling the assignment and the main reason why he came to this earth. He was about to pay a necessary price that would guarantee the redemption of the entire human race. Satan, knowing this truth, decided to take advantage of the curious nature of Peter to prevent Jesus from dying for our sins; just like he used the serpent in the Garden of Eden to relinquish power and dominion from Adam. Satan entered into Peter's heart because he was not yet born again at the time. Satan influenced him to rebuke Jesus Christ that He should not die to accomplish His assignment on earth .(out of the abundance of the heart the mouth speaks).

Knowing the exact personality operating behind the scene, Jesus addressed the situation from a spiritual point of view by dealing with Satan who had possessed Peter's heart. He said, "Satan, get behind me": "***23 But he turned, and said unto Peter, Get thee behind me, Satan: thou art an offence unto me: for thou savourest not the things that be of God, but those that be of men***" (Matthew 16:23). He did not say, "Peter, get behind me." Though Peter was actually standing before Jesus Christ at that particular moment, yet Satan spoke through him.

There are so many people in our world today, who, in their curiosity to search for God and know Him beyond the information that God has made available to us through His Word (the Bible), have entered into occultism, religion, worship of angels and idolatry. Satanic influence is real. Satan can manipulate anyone who is not born again to accomplish his evil agenda. He can also use a Christian who is still operating in the realms of ignorance of the Word of God to fulfill his evil plans.

In the trial of Satan, God did not allow him to speak in his defense because He is aware that Satan operates with three major influences:

1. Deception

    "***9 And the great dragon was cast out, that old serpent, called the Devil, and Satan, which deceiveth the whole world: he was cast out into the earth, and his angels were cast out with him***" (Revelation 12:9).

2. Accusation

    "***10 And I heard a loud voice saying in heaven, Now is come salvation, and strength, and the kingdom of our God, and the power of his Christ: for the accuser of our brethren is cast down, which accused them before our God day*** *and night"* (Revelation 12:10).

"1 And he showed me Joshua the high priest standing before the angel of the LORD, and Satan standing at his right hand to resist him. 2 And the LORD said unto Satan, The LORD rebuke thee, O Satan; even the LORD that hath chosen Jerusalem rebuke thee: is not this a brand plucked out of the fire? 3 Now Joshua was clothed with filthy garments, and stood before the angel" (Zachariah 3:1-3).

3. Lies

"44 Ye are of your father the devil, and the lusts of your father ye will do. He was a murderer from the beginning, and abode not in the truth, because there is no truth in him. When he speaketh a lie, he speaketh of his own: for he is a liar, and the father of it" (John 8:44).

Sometimes his accusation may be right against us, but the Supreme Court judge of heaven is a merciful God who will not be angry with His sons and daughters forever. It is evident that God did not allow Satan to open his defense because he is a liar and an accuser of God's children. You are not who Satan says you are, but you are who God says you are. Live with this consciousness and live a fear-free life.

The false evidence appeared so real to Eve that she could not resist when she saw the fruit (evidence). The mystery of Christianity was unfolded in the story of the fall of man – When Adam and Eve sinned by disobeying the voice of God, but obeyed the voice of Satan. Immediately, man moved from a spirit-centered being into carnality; from sinlessness to sinfulness; from righteousness to unrighteousness. They lost their right standing with God. Now, listen to the voice of God in Genesis 3:9; *"9 And the LORD God called unto Adam, and said unto him, Where art thou?"*

Adam and Eve misconstrued God's voice as the fear of punishment and anxiety over breaking God's law; which is the second category of fear called *'Yirathmalkul.'* Meanwhile, the voice was only an expression of love; the demonstration of love for the fallen man was in action. God was actually calling them to repentance and restoration. Why did God say, "Where are you?", as if He was not aware of their location at that moment. He was aware of where they were in the physical but He was only addressing their spiritual state at that moment – they have always been in the spirit, but this time around they had moved into carnality; so He was calling them out of the flesh back into the spirit where fellowship and relationship with Him could be possible again.

Nobody can worship God in the flesh (John 4:24). *"24 God is a Spirit: and they that worship him must worship him in spirit and in truth."* Our fellowship and relationship with God is spirit to spirit. This is the foundation of Christianity and this is why Christianity is completely different from religions. Christianity is: Man (or sinful man), where are you? Religion is: God, where are you? God is searching for sinful men and women through Jesus Christ; to save, restore and make them God's ambassadors upon the earth (2 Corinthians 5:18-20).

"18 And all things are of God, who hath reconciled us to himself by Jesus Christ, and hath given to us the ministry of reconciliation; 19 To wit, that God was in Christ, reconciling the world unto himself, not imputing their trespasses unto them; and hath committed unto us the word of reconciliation. 20 Now then we are ambassadors for Christ, as though God did beseech you by us: we pray you in Christ's stead, be ye reconciled to God."

- **Religion** is derived from the Latin word *'religio'* which means man's systems and ways of seeking and searching for God based on knowledge and not by faith in Christ Jesus. Man was made with a craving desire to worship and God did that with an intention for man to worship Him alone. After the fall of man, that desire was still in man, so man always desired to worship some deities. Now the devil, knowing this aspect of man's life, placed a demand on our innate desire for worship and he capitalized on our desire for worship to establish religion. This is the reason why there are so many religions in the world. Since the detachment of man from God from the beginning after the fall of man, man has looked for ways and systems based on false knowledge to get attached to God again. Satan is the chief architect behind all religions. Christianity is not a religion. In John 14:6, Jesus said, *"I am the way"* not a way. It means He is the one and only definite way — Jesus Christ is the way to the Father, not a truth but the definite and only truth that leads to the life of God which is the true life; the life of God (Zoe). In Jesus's dialogue with the Samaritan woman at the well, Jesus exposed a deeper truth about the kind of worship that God recognizes and duly accepts. Worship is not a slow rhythm gospel song, though worship song is an aspect of worship, but not worship in totality, now what is worship? It is a total dedication and devotion to God, and His kingdom. (e.g when you are committed to living a holy life, it's a worship, when you live a life of purity, sanctification, giving, it's worship. Abraham was not going to Mariah to sing songs of worship, but he went to offer Isaac as sacrifice to God , and he called that an act of worship. (**Genesis :22- 5) And Abraham said unto his young men, Abide ye here with the ass; and I and the lad will go yonder and worship, and come again to you.**) Jesus was not suggesting to the woman about this truth, but He placed an obligatory word "must " meaning it should not be overlooked or missed, **(John 4:24 God is a Spirit: and they that worship him must worship him in spirit and in truth)**. Those who desire to worship God "must " worship Him in spirit and in truth, that truth stands for Jesus Christ according to the Bible, and it's practically impossible to believe, confess and accept God's offer of salvation which is accessible through Christ without the conviction , and connectivity of the Holy Spirit. Holy Spirit is the personality that arrests the heart of sinners with a deep conviction before he or she can finally accept the truth which is Jesus Christ, Nobody can call Jesus Christ Lord except by the Holy Spirit (1 Corinthians 12:3) Any worship that is void of this truth is unacceptable to God, it's just a religion . Worshiping God through Jesus Christ based upon the conviction of the Holy Spirit is the only acceptable worship endorsed by God *"14 And the LORD God said unto the serpent, Because thou hast done this, thou art cursed above all cattle, and above every beast of the field; upon thy belly shalt thou go, and dust shalt thou eat all the days of thy life: 15 And I will put enmity between thee and the woman, and between thy seed and her seed; it shall bruise thy head, and thou shalt bruise his heel. 16 Unto the woman he said, I will greatly multiply thy sorrow and thy conception; in sorrow thou shalt bring forth children; and thy desire shall be to thy husband, and he shall rule over thee. 17 And unto Adam he said, Because thou hast hearkened unto the voice of thy wife, and hast eaten of the tree, of which I commanded thee, saying, Thou shalt not eat of it: cursed is the ground for thy sake; in sorrow shalt thou eat of it all the days of thy life"* (Genesis 3:14-17).

The love of God is so deep for mankind and that was why He displayed such a great love even for the fallen man . Though man disobeyed God through Satanic deception, the serpent was cursed because it allowed itself to be used by Satan, we ought to avoid being used by the devil to inflict pains, troubles, and hurts against our neighbours, so that we don't create generational curses for ourselves and the unborn generation. Man was not cursed, but the "ground" was cursed for man's sake. The ground was cursed for man's sake in order to execute His righteous judgment. God did not clear, acquit, or discharge man completely from the case of disobedience, but He exposed man to a difficult and hard condition which he had never experienced since creation. Man's disobedience exposed him to hardship, pains, difficulties, and also to the attacks and wickedness of the enemy. So, we also saw the compassion of a loving father in action – a father who could not watch His Children walk in nakedness. He decided to cover their shame and disgrace despite their sin. Are you troubled, guilty or ashamed because of your sins? Don't worry anymore!!! Because our loving father is still in the business of forgiveness, and He shall forgive you today no matter the gravity of your sin in Jesus name Amen. The love of God for mankind is greater than the love of every earthly parent towards his or her children. Even earthly parents, in our limitation and wickedness, still know how to give good gifts to our children; how much more our heavenly father, full of love, mercy, and compassion?

13 If ye then, being evil, know how to give good gifts unto your children: how much more shall your heavenly Father give the Holy Spirit to them that ask him?" (Luke 11:13).

God did not drive Adam and Eve out of the Garden of Eden as punishment, No! God doesn't punish His children, but He disciplines them with an intention to correct them, so that they can constantly walk in righteousness (Hebrews 12: 5 -11) . He actually did that for man's sake. Please note that the Garden of Eden was not a place but an atmosphere called "delight" It's not a place, though it is vastly believed wrongly that the garden of Eden is situated in the Middle East somewhere near where these Rivers are today (Tigris and Euphrates) .Remember that in that Garden was not only the tree of knowledge of good and evil, but it also consists the tree of life. (Genesis 2:17): ***"17 But of the tree of the knowledge of good and evil, thou shalt not eat of it: for in the day that thou eatest thereof thou shalt surely die."*** They were introduced to the most dangerous dimension of life: Having the knowledge of good and evil, but they lacked the ability to do good, and to rightly judge, because their consciences and heart had been tainted with disobedience as a result of the wrong information they received through Satanic deception.

They had wrong and evil information ; so their minds and hearts were inclined towards doing evil. They could not stand in the atmosphere of "Delight" with this mindset and fallen state. Delight means something that gives great pleasure, satisfaction or happiness. Delight symbolizes Heaven, a place of peace, joy, and love.

It also symbolizes a place of safety and order, acceptance and love. It is practically impossible to live in the atmosphere of pleasure, satisfaction, and happiness with evil mindset, corrupt and polluted heart and mind. Eden symbolizes Heaven, so no evil can dwell in Heaven; a place of peace, love, joy and orderliness. After their act of disobedience, Adam and Eve's lives and position were in disorder.

"22 And the LORD God said, Behold, the man is become as one of us, to know good and evil: and now, lest he put forth his hand, and take also of the tree of life, and eat, and live forever" (Genesis 3:22).

In the Garden of Eden was the tree of life. That tree of life symbolizes Jesus Christ who is the eternal life. God had to move them from the Garden of Eden to a different place and atmosphere in order to prevent them from having access to the tree of life. Man would have eaten the tree of life in that fallen state if God did not move them out, and that would have resulted in a complete woe for man; in that, the fallen man would not be different from Satan who cannot be forgiven again. He is already destined for destruction and his destination is hell fire. If there was another remedy for the fallen man even if he ate the tree of life, God would not have driven them out of the Garden. It would have been impossible for man to die with Christ on the Cross in order for him to live again with God.

CHAPTER FOUR

ELEVEN COMMON TYPES OF DEMONIC FEAR

1. **FEAR OF DEATH:** Fear of death is sometimes referred to as *'thanatophobia'*. This word is derived from the Greek word *'thanatos'* which means the god of death, and *'phobos'* means fear. The fear of death is the persistent natural thought of death to us. The spirit behind the fear of death is the spirit that engineers suicidal thoughts. This kind of fear kills even before death arrives because of the intense phobia. Some people who could have escaped death from disease actually died because of fear. Nobody commits suicide without experiencing a persistent thought of committing suicide. If the thought keeps on coming, and nothing is done to combat it, it ends up producing suicidal death (Hebrews 2:14-15).

"14 Forasmuch then as the children are partakers of flesh and blood, he also himself likewise took part of the same; that through death he might destroy him that had the power of death, that is, the devil; 15 And deliver them who through fear of death were all their lifetime subject to bondage."

FOUR KINDS OF DEATH

1. Physical death
2. Spiritual death to God
3. Spiritual death to sin, Satan, and self
4. Eternal death

The mystery of death: Death is not a threat to a Christian and it is pointless for a Christian to be afraid of death. Apostle Paul said, for him to die is gain. He desired to leave his body of sin. That means he yearned to transit from this world to the other in order to be with the Lord. Death is not a loss to a Christian; rather, it is a great gain, because it is an opportunity to be with the Lord. The greatest achievement in life is to accept Jesus Christ and endeavor to make it to heaven and be with the Lord forever. How long are we going to live on this earth? This earth is full of sorrows, oppression and injustice. But we have a better place where there will be no sorrow, pain, weeping, injustice and death (Psalm

116:15): *"15 Precious in the sight of the LORD is the death of his saints."* Precious is the death of a Christian in the sight of God; if the death of a Christian is pleasing to God, then it means it is truly a great gain. If so, why are we still afraid of death?

There are four kinds of death:

1. Physical death
2. Spiritual death to God
3. Spiritual death to sin, Satan and self
4. Eternal death

1. **Physical death** It is a separation of the soul from he body, this death was introduced by Adam through disobedience to the Word of God (Romans 5:12-14): *"12 Wherefore, as by one man sin entered into the world, and death by sin; and so death passed upon all men, for that all have sinned: 13 (For until the law sin was in the world: but sin is not imputed when there is no law. 14 Nevertheless death reigned from Adam to Moses, even over them that had not sinned after the similitude of Adam's transgression, who is the figure of him that was to come."*

   This kind of death reigns over all mankind because we all have sinned (Romans 3:23); *"23 For all have sinned, and come short of the glory of God."* The moment Adam sinned against the Word of the Lord, the consequence of Adam's action came into play (Genesis 2:17): *"17 But of the tree of the knowledge of good and evil, thou shalt not eat of it: for in the day that thou eatest thereof thou shalt surely die."*

   "Thou shall surely die" immediately took effect, but Adam did not die a physical death at that moment but that death was already set in motion and he was waiting for his expiry date on this earth, even though that was not the original plan of God for mankind., **(Genesis 3:19) In the sweat of thy face shalt thou eat bread, till thou return unto the ground; for out of it wast thou taken: for dust thou art, and unto dust shalt thou return.** God actually had a plan for man to live forever, but not to live forever in sin and disobedience (Genesis 3:22): *"22 And the LORD God said, Behold, the man is become as one of us, to know good and evil: and now, lest he put forth his hand, and take also of the tree of life, and eat, and live forever:"* The tree of life now became the only hope for man to live forever and Jesus Christ is that tree of life (John 15:1-2): 15:1, **I am the true vine, and my Father is the husbandman.15:2 Every branch in me that beareth not fruit he taketh away: and every branch that beareth fruit, he purgeth it, that it may bring forth more fruit**. and we Christians are described as His branches. It means He is truly the tree of life in the Garden of Eden.

2. **Spiritual Death to God** is the act of detaching and separating from God's kind of life, plan and purpose. Though someone who's dead to God will still have blood flowing in his vessels signifying that he is physically alive, but that person is blind and dead in the sight of God. There are lots of intellectual, influential, rich and wealthy people who are living physically and walking about receiving honor and worldly awards, but they are spiritually blind and dead. The good news to the people who are spiritually dead and blind, but not physically dead, is that there is hope of resurrection – hope of coming back to life. This will be expanded in the third point below, which is:

3. **Spiritual Death to Sin, Self and Satan:**

    This spiritual death is simply dying with Jesus Christ, and this death occurs and is set in motion the day we accept Jesus Christ as our Lord and Savior. When Jesus Christ died and was buried, He resurrected. Anyone who accepts the life of God through the acceptance of Jesus Christ automatically experiences the death, burial, and resurrection with Jesus Christ.

    20 Wherefore if ye be dead with Christ from the rudiments of the world, why, as though living in the world, are ye subject to ordinances"

    (Colossians 2:20).

    "20 I am crucified with Christ: nevertheless I live; yet not I, but Christ liveth in me: and the life which I now live in the flesh I live by the faith of the Son of God, who loved me, and gave himself for me" (Galatians 2:20).

    "12 Buried with him in baptism, wherein also ye are risen with him through the faith of the operation of God, who hath raised him from the dead" (Colossians 2:12).

    "1 If ye then be risen with Christ, seek those things which are above, where Christ sitteth on the right hand of God" (Colossians 3:1).

This kind of death gives you the advantage to reign over sin, Satan, self and natural death. Paul puts it this way: "I die daily".

(Romans 6: 7- 12) 6:7 For he that is dead is freed from sin.6:8 Now if we be dead with Christ, we believe that we shall also live with him:6:9 Knowing that Christ being raised from the dead dieth no more; death hath no more dominion over him.6:10 For in that he died, he died unto sin once: but in that he liveth, he liveth unto God.6:11 Likewise reckon ye also yourselves to be dead indeed unto sin, but alive unto God through Jesus Christ our Lord.6:12 Let not sin therefore reign in your mortal body, that ye should obey it in the lusts.

thereof.

("*14 If a man die, shall he live again? all the days of my appointed time will I wait, till my change come*" (Job 14:14). The question of Job can only be answered adequately on the basis of divine revelation. If a man dies, can hbe live again? There are two kinds of man:

1. The Natural Man
2. The Spirit Man

In Job's dispensation, if a natural man dies, he cannot live again because Jesus Christ has not died physically on the cross to pay the debt of the sins of the whole world, even though by the authority of the scripture , He had already been slain in other words He had already been sacrificed before the foundation of the world . Those who are qualify to live again in eternity with God in that dispensation, are those who slept (Died) through faith in anticipation of the coming messiah Jesus Christ.

"*8 And all that dwell upon the earth shall worship him, whose names are not written in the book of life of the Lamb slain from the foundation of the world*" (Revelation 13:8). Job spoke based on the revelation available to Him at the time.

A natural man is born of the flesh, and a spirit man is born of the spirit (John 3:6): "*6 That which is born of the flesh is flesh; and that which is born of the Spirit is spirit.*" A natural man can still live again if he does not die physically by transiting from this world. The only way the natural man can escape the physical and eternal death is to contact the life of God, which is ZOE, by accepting Jesus Christ as his Lord and Savior. The Holy Spirit does three major works in the lives of non-Christians:

1. He convicts the heart of the non-Christian

   "37 Now when they heard this, they were pricked in their heart, and said unto Peter and to the rest of the apostles, Men and brethren, what shall we do? 38 Then Peter said unto them, Repent, and be baptized every one of you in the name of Jesus Christ for the remission of sins, and ye shall receive the gift of the Holy Ghost" (Acts 2:37-38).

   "12 I have yet many things to say unto you, but ye cannot bear them now" (John 16:12).

   The Holy Spirit has the power and ability to convert the heart of any sinner, no matter how sinful or rebellious they are. This is why we are sometimes amazed at how notorious murderers, armed robbers, and prostitutes can surrender to the lordship of Jesus Christ without compulsion. No sinner can confess the lordship of Jesus Christ unless he or she is called by God and influenced through the conviction of the Holy Spirit.

   "11 But if the Spirit of him that raised up Jesus from the dead dwell in you, he that raised up Christ from the dead shall also quicken your mortal bodies by his Spirit that dwelleth in you" (Romans 8:11).

2. The Holy Spirit quickens our mortal bodies; in other words, the Holy Spirit quickens our dead lives which can also be referred to as ordinary life – this is what Jesus accomplished on the cross. He took our death and gave us life, which is ZOE; the life of God. The moment the Holy Spirit comes to reside in you, there is change of location; you are immediately moved from death to life. Hallelujah!!!

3. *"13 Howbeit when he, the Spirit of truth, is come, he will guide you into all truth: for he shall not speak of himself; but whatsoever he shall hear, that shall he speak: and he will show you things to come"*

   (John 16:13).

"14 For as many as are led by the Spirit of God, they are the sons of God"

(Romans 8:14).

After the experience of salvation by the order of being born again, the Holy Spirit is responsible for teaching, guiding, and leading the sons and daughters of God. The Holy Spirit cannot teach, lead or guide the non-Christian into all truth; that is why they ignorantly operate in partial truth that Jesus is only a prophet. It is pointless wasting time trying to teach a non-Christian about the fact that Jesus is God. He cannot accept or understand such a mystery because such mysteries are spiritually discerned.

Apostle Paul puts it this way; that "those who sleep in the Lord..." Christians don't die but we sleep in the Lord (1 Corinthian 15:51-52).

"51 Behold, I show you a mystery; We shall not all sleep, but we shall all be changed, 52 In a moment, in the twinkling of an eye, at the last trump: for the trumpet shall sound, and the dead shall be raised incorruptible, and we shall be changed."

Jesus will appear with His angels with a great shout and trumpet for two reasons:

"16 For the Lord himself shall descend from heaven with a shout, with the voice of the archangel, and with the trump of God: and the dead in Christ shall rise first: 17 Then we which are alive and remain shall be caught up together with them in the clouds, to meet the Lord in the air: and so shall we ever be with the Lord. 18 Wherefore comfort one another with these words" (1 Thessalonians 4:16-18).

(1) To create awareness for the entire world to see Him, including those who pierced him, (Revelation 1:7): ***"7 Behold, he cometh with clouds; and every eye shall see him, and they also which pierced him: and all kindreds of the earth shall wail because of him. Even so, Amen."*** Those who pierced Him are symbolic of those who remain in sin or fail to accept God's offer of Salvation.

(2) No matter how deep we sleep, the moment we hear noise, we wake up – dead people cannot wake up no matter the gravity of the noise around them. If you are a Christian, I submit to you that you cannot die again, You only sleep in the Lord,. so stop being afraid of death.

Two Kinds of Men:

The ordinary man with an ordinary life called ***bios*** in Greek – that life has eternal death already placed on it as a result of the disobedience of Adam. Eternity is in two fold : eternal life and eternal death – both lives begin here on earth. Eternal death can be cancelled when eternal life enters into it but if eternal life doesn't enter such a life, that life will transit from this earth after the physical death, and continue its eternity in Hell Fire. Eternal life is the life of God. This life is resurrection and life – this life knows no failure or boundaries; it is the life of God. He that has the ordinary life came into this world through human conception (sexual intercourse). This man is carnal, devoid of the spirit of God.

The other man is a spirit man, born by the Spirit of God. He that is born of the Spirit is Spirit. Such a man is a spirit. He died once with Christ on the cross, buried with Christ, and resurrected with Christ. Since it is appointed for man to die once, he had already died and can die no more - He now lives in the faith of Christ forever. This man has two eyes, two legs, two hands, but does not see things with those eyes anymore. He does not walk with those legs anymore. He does not have to touch first, like Thomas, before believing anymore. He walks, sees, and touches by faith. He can be at a particular location and see into the future like Abraham. His eyes could see his great possession from the ordinary to the supernatural.

The Mystery of Death:

Death is gain to a believer. The reason why Jesus says He will come with His archangels and a shout and noise is simply because no matter how deep anyone sleeps, the moment he or she hears a shout, he will surely wake up. Christians don't die, we sleep, and when Jesus comes, we shall rise again. **Hallelujah!!!**

2. **FEAR OF THE FUTURE** is termed as *'Chronophobia'*. This word is derived from the Greek word *'Chronos'* which means time; and phobia means fear. This kind of fear is the persistent and irrational fear that time is passing by. This fear compels people to make wrong decisions because they feel time is catching up with them. Some of these decisions are visible in marriages, childbirth, finances, academic pursuits, etc. Satan always deploys uncertain pictures of our future to manipulate our minds to take quick negative actions in order to escape the uncertain future

that he has revealed to us. *Meanwhile God is speaking to His children through His words here :*

"11 For I know the thoughts that I think toward you, saith the LORD, thoughts of peace, and not of evil, to give you an expected end" (Jeremiah 29:11).

Anxieties and worries have no shape or form, but we can only imagine them in our minds. For instance, what will I eat today? What will I wear? How will my future be? These are all that the Bible calls, the "cares of life." You cannot see all these things, but they can cause you to be sick or broken, FEAR NOT!

Instead of being worried about things we don't see, which are not even the realities of life, Philippians 4:8 suggests what we should be thinking about: *"8 Finally, brethren, whatsoever things are true, whatsoever things are honest, whatsoever things are just, whatsoever things are pure, whatsoever things are lovely, whatsoever things are of good report; if there be any virtue, and if there be any praise, think on these things."*

The first word on the list of these biblical prescriptions, which is truth, depicts that any other thing which falls short of the truth of God's Word for your life is not worthy of thinking about. No wonder the Bible says elsewhere in Proverbs 23:7 that, *"7 For as he thinketh in his heart, so is he: Eat and drink, saith he to thee; but his heart is not with thee."* Any lie of the devil you think and worry about everyday will surely come to pass if you don't deal with it. Instead of thinking and worrying about those lies, God is saying you should rather think about things that are true, honest, just (righteousness), pure, lovely, of good report, virtuous, and praise-worthy; so that you can produce the right results in your life. You may not know what the future holds for you but that shouldn't be a cause for worry. Just try as much as possible to know the One who knows all things about your future. His name is Alpha and Omega. He knows the end from the beginning.

3. The **FEAR OF MARRIAGE** is termed *'Gametophobia'*; derived from the Greek word 'gamete' (wife) and *'gamein'* (to marry). These two words in English language refer to two types of cells that come together in reproduction to begin formation of embryo in females. These cells are called eggs in females and spermatozoa (sperms) in males. Fear of marriage is an abnormal and persistent fear of being married, though marriage based on God's principles pose no threat. They fear the challenges and the responsibilities of rearing a family; they

sometimes accommodate the fear of failing as a sexual partner. Some are afraid of suffering disappointment which might lead to a broken home as a result of divorce – no one in his or her right frame of mind will enter a relationship with the same gender, but the fear of marriage is the demonic foolery behind such a decision.

Some people are afraid of getting married because of the negative experiences of friends, families, or even their own past experiences in their past relationships. Therefore, they prefer, out of their will, to remain single in order to avoid such a situation from occurring in their marriages. Meanwhile, God's plan for His sons and daughters concerning marriage is for them to come together (male and female) (Genesis 2:18) to live joyfully and to help each other to fulfil their God-given assignments on earth. Because everybody needs somebody, a man needs a woman, and the woman also needs the man; because two are better than one (Ecclesiastes 4:9-10).

4. The **FEAR OF POVERTY** is *'Peniaphobia'*. The word *'penia'* is Greek, and it means poverty, and *phobos* in Greek means fear. The increase of crime in our world today is directly connected to the demonic activities empowered by the spirit of the fear of poverty. Bribery and corruption, greed, love of money, selfishness, etc. are all evil practices borne out of the fear of poverty. This kind of fear denies so many people the opportunity to enjoy the financial blessings of God. Satan devises this fear with an intent to perpetually attach his victims to himself for destruction. This kind of fear propels people to do all kinds of wicked things just with an intent to escape poverty. Many people have dipped their hands into the wickedness of money rituals where human beings are used for sacrifice.

"17 And when he was gone forth into the way, there came one running, and kneeled to him, and asked him, Good Master, what shall I do that I may inherit eternal life? 18 And Jesus said unto him, Why callest thou me good? Tthere is none good but one, that is, God. 19 Thou knowest the commandments, Do not commit adultery, Do not kill, Do not steal, Do not bear false witness, Defraud not, Honour thy father and mother. 20 And he answered and said unto him, Master, all these have I observed from my youth. 21 Then Jesus beholding him loved him, and said unto him, One thing thou lackest: go thy way, sell whatsoever thou hast, and give to the poor, and thou shalt have treasure in heaven: and come, take up the cross, and follow me. 22 And he was sad at that

saying, and went away grieved: for he had great possessions. 23 And Jesus looked round about, and saith unto his disciples, How hardly shall they that have riches enter into the kingdom of God! 24 And the disciples were astonished at his words. But Jesus answereth again, and saith unto them, Children, how hard is it for them that trust in riches to enter into the kingdom of God! 25 It is easier for a camel to go through the eye of a needle, than for a rich man to enter into the kingdom of God. 26 And they were astonished out of measure, saying among themselves, Who then can be saved? 27 And Jesus looking upon them saith, With men it is impossible, but not with God: for with God all things are possible. 28 Then Peter began to say unto him, Lo, we have left all, and have followed thee. 29 And Jesus answered and said, Verily I say unto you, There is no man that hath left house, or brethren, or sisters, or father, or mother, or wife, or children, or lands, for my sake, and the gospel's, 30 But he shall receive an hundredfold now in this time, houses, and brethren, and sisters, and mothers, and children, and lands, with persecutions; and in the world to come eternal life" (Mark 10:17-30).

A rich young man ran to Jesus kneeling down before him. He had great possession but he was not satisfied because something important was lacking in his life. We could see clearly from his response to Jesus' questions that the young man had been an obedient student to the law and the commandments right from his youth yet he lacked something important. This means that we can be obedient to the laws of God and yet not have eternal life. This rich young man had obeyed the laws of God from his youth. It means that he had not stolen, defrauded, fornicated or committed adultery from his youth, yet he was still a sinner because he had no eternal life. We reads in 1 John 5:20 that, *"20 And we know that the Son of God is come, and hath given us an understanding, that we may know him that is true, and we are in him that is true, even in his Son Jesus Christ. This is the true God, and eternal life"*.

If Christ is in you, then you have eternal life. Eternal life does not begin when you leave the earth, but when you accept the life of God, which is ZOE.

"6 And hath raised us up together, and made us sit together in heavenly places in Christ Jesus." (Ephesians 2:6).

In this scripture, the Bible did not say we shall sit with Christ, but we are already seated with Him in heavenly places. Eternal life is far more exceedingly valuable than all the riches, wealth, and possessions of this life. Jesus wanted the rich young man to value eternal life much more than all the possession he had acquired. This young man wrongly thought that eternal life is an introduction to a poor life. He left the presence of Jesus Christ (eternal life) without laying hold on eternal life which consists of greater riches, wealth and possession more than what he actually possessed which has no eternal value.

"12 Fight the good fight of faith, lay hold on eternal life, whereunto thou art also called, and hast professed a good profession before many witnesses" (1 Timothy 6:12).

This man's action propelled Jesus to make a shocking statement which greatly astonished his disciples. Why were they surprised? They were astonished because they had also left all their possession and followed Jesus. They did exactly what the young man could not do.

"23 And Jesus looked round about, and saith unto his disciples, How hardly shall they that have riches enter into the kingdom of God!" (Mark 10:23)

Jesus says it is easy for a camel to pass through the eye of the needle. I have heard a lot of preachers saying that Jesus was talking about a literal gate. They say that Jerusalem is a great city in Israel; a walled city with a large gate; within the large gate is a smaller gate called the eye of a needle. Whenever the main gate is shut at a specific time in the evening, that the only entry point will be through the smaller gate – eye of a needle. It is called the eye of a needle because it can only permit one person's entrance at a time. Two camels cannot pass through this gate at a time. The owner of the camel would also have to drop down from the camel to allow it to go in first, before he would follow suit. If there are goods on the camel, it means the rich men who used camels those days took their time to offload the goods on the camel, send them through the gates one by one, the camel follows after before the rich man could enter. Though this explanation sounds interesting, yet there is no archeological evidence that such a gate ever existed. What this illustration simply means is that no possession can follow you to the Kingdom of God. Those who trust in their riches and possessions have to drop them; the word here is "trust "otherwise, it will be hard for them to enter into the Kingdom of God.

Jesus used that illustration to explain how it is impossible for those who esteem the riches of this world more than the gift of eternal life (JESUS) to enter into God's Kingdom. It is absolutely impossible for Jesus to call anyone to follow him with an intention to make the person poor. No!!! He was rich yet He died poor; so that through His poverty we might be rich (2 Corinthians 8:9). So, we can safely say that Jesus has something far better and more valuable to offer to the rich young man which is far greater in value than whatever he possessed. Jesus would have caused this man to experience kingdom riches and prosperity because the earth is the Lord's and the fullness thereof (Psalm 24:1), and he would have also received the most valuable asset anyone could ever possess on this earth, and that is eternal life; but this man ignorantly rejected eternal life due to his mundane possessions. Jesus made this demand of the rich young man to know the condition of his heart concerning his possession. Jesus knew that the heart of the rich young man was outrightly glued to his possession and that was why He asked him to sell all his possession and come follow Him. Jesus did not want this man or anyone who desires to follow him to have a divided heart, and divided attention. Your heart will always remain where your treasure is (Matthew 6:21) **"For where your treasure is, there will your heart be also."** Jesus needed his whole heart to fully follow Him in love (Matthew 22:37): **"37 Jesus said unto him, Thou shalt love the Lord thy God with all thy heart, and with all thy soul, and with all thy mind."**

No one can serve two masters. He will either love one orand hate the other. You cannot serve God with your heart full of love for him and also serve money at the same time with the same heart (Matthew 6:24), **"24 No man can serve two masters: for either he will hate the one, and love the other; or else he will hold to the one, and despise the other. Ye cannot serve God and mammon."** That is why it is impossible to genuinely love two wives, girlfriends, or boyfriends at the same time. Following Jesus requires our undivided love for Him and that is when the promise of God in one1 (1 Corinthians 2:9) can become a reality in our lives.

Jesus painted a picture with this illustration that just as it is impossible for a camel to go through the eye of a needle., Iit is also impossible for any rich or wealthy person whose heart is tied to the riches of this world to enter into the Kingdom of God, unless the person accepts God's offer of Salvation which is accessible through believing and confessing Jesus Christ as his Lord and Savior. That is why Jesus said being born again is impossible with men no matter their possession, but such a miracle of new birth can only be possible with God through Jesus

Christ.

Nevertheless, if only they will accept God's plan of Salvation through Jesus Christ, they will surely enter into the Kingdom in spite of their possession. The disciples were astonished. They began to ask questions among themselves. 'WHO THEN CAN BE SAVED?' This question suggests that Jesus' disciples were aware of the true riches, prosperity and great possession which haves been made available for us through the finished work of Christ Jesus at the Cross, but they were a bit confused simply because of what Jesus said. He said Tthat, it is hard for rich men to enter into the Kingdom of God. Out of curiosity, Peter, who left a large fishing business behind for the sake of following Jesus, exclaimed with a loud voice; "We have left all and followed you!" Peter was trying to find out the earthly benefit for following Jesus Christ. This means that even though Peter had followed Jesus for more than 3 years, yet he was still engulfed with the fear of poverty. So, Jesus quickly responded to him, and gave him an adequate answer that should give every Christian the assurance of the victory that we have obtained over poverty. Though this victory has been established, yet many Christians are still walking in ignorance by failing to access the riches and prosperity that the death, burial, and the resurrection of Jesus made available to us.

You can get a copy of my book, **UNLEASHING GOD'S AGENDA OF PROSPERITY**. In this book, you will be enlightened with an in-depth information about the prosperity plan of God for the Christian and how you can access Kingdom riches and prosperity without struggle.

Remember that prior to Jesus' encounter with the rich young man, Peter was faced with a similar examination which he passed by giving an adequate answer to Jesus' question (John 6:66,68); *"66 From that time many of his disciples went back, and walked no more with him.", "68 Then Simon Peter answered him, Lord, to whom shall we go? thou hast the words of eternal life."* But in the second examination, the question was extremely difficult for him to answer. The Bible says "they were astonished out of measure", meaning they had a feeling of great surprise and wonder concerning the topic of the benefits of following Jesus. So Jesus had to quickly expound the topic to broaden their scope of understanding on the subject of Kingdom benefits. In verse 29-30, Jesus explained: "No man." It means that nobody is exempted from this benefit provided he or she is ready to follow Jesus according to the principle of undivided heart and attention. The first statement on the list of benefits for following Jesus should be reasonable enough to settle the issue that is vastly believed by many Christians that Christianity offers no earthly benefit but only eternal life. Those who believe in this assertion dwell on the platform of half-truth. That was why Jesus explained this truth in detail. In the **verse 30 of Mark chapter 10**, Jesus made it very clear that those who follow Him wholeheartedly would receive hundred fold of blessings "NOW" in this time, and He concluded this verse by saying that such people would also enjoy eternal life in the world to come. That eternal life begins from NOW and it continues to eternity. eternal life is the ultimate gift that the death of Jesus offers, yet the death, burial and resurrection of Jesus actually offers the Christian immeasurable benefits apart from what Jesus listed in Mark 10:29-30.

"29 And Jesus answered and said, Verily I say unto you, There is no man that hath left house, or brethren, or sisters, or father, or mother, or wife, or children, or lands, for my sake, and the gospel's, 30 But he shall receive an hundredfold now in this time, houses, and brethren, and sisters, and mothers, and children, and lands, with persecutions; and in the world to come eternal life."

Let's read Revelation 5:10-12 for more clarification: *"10 And hast made us unto our God kings and priests: and we shall reign on the earth. 11 And I beheld, and I heard the voice of many angels round about the throne and the beasts and the elders: and the number of them was ten thousand times ten thousand, and thousands of thousands; 12 Saying with a loud voice, Worthy is the Lamb that was slain to receive power, and riches, and wisdom, and strength, and honor, and glory, and blessing."*

All the benefits listed in these verses are at the disposal of the Christian. But it is pointless to have all the listed earthly benefits but lose eternity Iin heaven with God; that is an irrevocable loss. The destiny of such a person is hell fire.

"36 For what shall it profit a man, if he shall gain the whole world, and lose his own soul? 37 Or what shall a man give in exchange for his soul? 38 Whosoever therefore shall be ashamed of me and of my words in this adulterous and sinful generation; of him also shall the Son of man be ashamed, when he cometh in the glory of his Father with the holy angels" (Mark 8:36-38).

Jesus went to hell so that you will not have to go to hell anymore.

"18 For Christ also hath once suffered for sins, the just for the unjust, that he might bring us to God, being put to death in the flesh, but quickened by the Spirit: 19 By which also he went and preached unto the spirits in prison; 20 Which sometime were disobedient, when once the longsuffering of God waited in the days of Noah, while the ark was a preparing, wherein few, that is, eight souls were saved by water" (1 Peter 3:18-20).

Christ's birth, death, and resurrection wereas purposely for two significant reasons:

- For our example; to follow Him in righteousness. That means to pattern our lives the way He lived on this earth.
- For exchange; He came to exchange our curses for blessings; diseases for health; death for life; poverty for riches; weakness for strength.

If God can offer His only Son to give us eternal life, is it possession that He cannot give us a hundred times? That is why the scripture says all things are yours.

"32 He that spared not his own Son, but delivered him up for us all, how shall he not with him also freely give us all things?" (Romans 8:32)

5. **FEAR OF CONTRACTING DISEASES:** This fear in Greek is called *"Nosophobia"*; "noses" is for disease and "phobia" means fear in Greek. This kind of fear manipulates our minds to live in the fear or bondage of contracting one disease or the other. There is nothing wrong with being careful to avoid contracting diseases; by taking good care of yourself, eating healthy, living healthy, and avoiding anything that could possibly hazard your health life:

but it actually becomes a deadly issue when we live under such fear of contracting diseases. Living in such fear will deny us the opportunity to enjoying life in total freedom from sicknesses and diseases that God has freely given to us through the death and resurrection of our Lord Jesus Christ (Isaiah 53:5).

Fear of sicknesses and diseases is similar to the fear of deatthdeath in manifestation. There are families who battle a particular kind of sickness or disease, like stroke, diabetes, cancer, etc. The devil will always take an undue advantage of what we perceive to be real as a result of prior evidence to manipulate us into accommodating fear which will end up producing the expected result that the devil desires.

6. **FEAR OF SIN** is termed *"Hamartophobia."* The origin of the word *"hamarto"* is Greek, and it means sin, and phobos means fear in Greek. This kind of fear makes us fear sin instead of having reverential fear for God. It is absolutely right to hate, rebel and refuse sin in our lives, but it will become a bondage when we are enslaved by the fear of sin. (You ought to fear God by hating sin, but don't live under the bondage of fear of sin).

Christ's obedience to die for our sin gives us victory over the power of sin. Instead of being afraid of sin, exercise your dominion over sin through the power of the Holy Spirit who is in you. Apostle Paul, under the inspiration of the Holy Spirit, declares that sin shall not have dominion over us (Romans 6:12-14). SHALL is an expression of command or obligation. Paul brought to our consciousness the obligation we have as Christians to rebel against sin. Under normal circumstances, anything you are afraid of will surely have dominion over you. We are obliged to stop living in the consciousness of sin; otherwise, sin will continue to dominate our mind, heart, and life. When Jesus said, "It is finished" on the cross, that declaration includes freedom from sin, self, and Satan.

I was also a victim of the fear of sin while growing up as a Muslim. I was addicted to all kinds of hard drugs. I did all I could to stop but to no avail. I always lived in the fear of committing this error. I sometimes took hard decisions to quit, but the spirit of fear of sin was already established in my heart and enslaved me to this sinful habit. But after being born again in the prison, I got myself engaged in the knowledge of God's Word, and I was possessed with the consciousness of who I am in Christ Jesus like the prodigal son in (Luke 15:17-18) I decided to follow Jesus Christ, and surprisingly, that urge for drugs suddenly disappeared without even praying about it.

Christians have been empowered to reign over sin, flesh, and Satan and not to be afraid of sin. The reason is because we cannot reign over what we are afraid of. The day a king or president begins to live in the fear of his subjects, he automatically loses his authority. Sin is not the lifestyle of the new creature in Christ Jesus, and that is why we feel guilty anytime we err even if nobody is aware.

When we err, we feel guilty not because God, or the Holy Spirit, condemns us, but we feel guilty and regret because that is not the lifestyle of a new creature in Christ Jesus. We have been born into a Holy Family so we ought to live by the standard of Holiness of Christ Jesus.

When you are engulfed in the fear of sin, recognize that it is from Satan. He puts you under the bondage of what you have been empowered to overcome. You need to focus on the right thoughts and refuse to fear. You ought to stop living in the consciousness of sin, or it will continue to have dominion over you.

Sin is not conducive in the life of a new creation in Christ Jesus. So, that is why when a Christian falls into sin, the person will immediately lose his or her joy and peace; the Holy Spirit will reprove him/her of his/her sin. He will not possibly condemn or judge him, but he or she cannot be comfortable. Whereas the life of sin is a normal thing to a sinner. That is his lifestyle; he doesn't even feel guilty or ashamed. I was surprised to see a certain young man caught in the act of homosexuality in the prison, and he was comfortably playing football the next morning without any sign of shyness or shame. The first step to overcoming sin, self and Satan is to be BORN AGAIN, and the second essential step that enable you to enjoying your Christian life is SELF REALIZATION. The prodigal son would have ended up in perpetual misery if he didn't come to the point of SELF REALIZATION. Until you realize who you are in Christ Jesus, you are not set to live a dignified life. The death of Jesus Christ has positioned you in the royalty of God, and as a honorable king, you are not permitted to live a dishonorable life, a responsible king can never live below the standard of his kingdom, kings don't misbehave. You ought to arrive at this point in your Christian life, where you will understand that he that is born of the king of kings (GOD) cannot sin (1 John 3:9). Remember that any unconfessed, and un forsaken sin will lead to eternal death in hell fire.

7. **FEAR OF DEFEAT:** Is there any situation you are going through that seems that you cannot overcome? God has already declared us victors in Christ Jesus. No situation can prevail against a child of God who is endowed with divine information of where he/she is in Christ Jesus. Is it imprisonment, sadness, diseases, pain, lack, disappointment? All these challenges come into our lives so that we can depend on the victory package embedded in God's Word. The fear of failure always makes negative room for people to concede to defeat in the pursuit of their lives' goals even when God has given them victory. No situation can see your end because you have been given a divine mandate to prevail over all situations. Do not be afraid (Revelation 2:10) ; *2:10 Fear none of those things*

which thou shalt suffer: behold, the devil shall cast some of you into prison, that ye may be tried; and ye shall have tribulation ten days: be thou faithful unto death, and I will give thee a crown of life.

That situation will not kill you in Jesus' name. Don't allow the fear of the situation to deny you of your right in Christ Jesus. You are more than a conqueror in Jesus name, Amen. .

8. **The FEAR OF FAILURE** is termed *"atychiphobia".* The devil employs this kind of fear to sabotage our chances of becoming successful in life. This kind of fear stands between us and our goals; it is an intense worry we experience whenever we imagine all the horrible things that could possibly happen to us if we fail to achieve our goal. The fear of failure always makes negative room for people to concede defeat in the pursuit of life's goals even when God has given them victory. Many gifted and talented people are mostly victims of this kind of phobia. They fail to utilize their God-given abilities due to the fear of failure which they have accommodated. Many people have stopped pursuing business ideas that would have led to unusual breakthroughs just because they are afraid of failing in business. Some stopped pursuing education because they are scared of failing in their academic pursuit. Those who are afraid of failing cannot experience success. The servant with one talent failed to utilize his talent because he was afraid of failing in investment. Meanwhile, the servants with two and five talents became successful and experienced increase because they did not allow the fear of failing to deny them the opportunity to succeed.

My son, Precious, was so ambitious to study accounting in the University. He kept on repeating this to me anytime I asked him about what he would like to become in future. He wrote his West African Examination Council's examination and made a distinction. He wrote his JAMB and also got a perfect result. Then he wrote the final examination that would determine his entrance to the university of his choice. Unfortunately, he could not make up to the required mark in that examination. He got 12 marks instead of 15; so he had to write this exam the following year. He refreshed for the exam but decided to change the university of his choice and his program of accounting. He changed from accounting to business management.

Why the sudden change contrary to the accounting he had sung to my hearing all his life? It is because he was afraid of failure; he decided to run away from the ambition to settle for something less which he considered easy to cope with. There is no dream, vision, and ambition too big or too difficult to realize if only you will not give up. I later encouraged him to remain focused on his desire to read accounting and he later made it because he did not give up.

It is said that Thomas Edison and his team of researchers tested more than 3,000 designs for the electric light bulb between 1878 and 1880. He never gave up on his dream of making an electric light bulb. Imagine if he had given up on that particular dream, and decided to shift his focus to making microphone; he would have died without realizing his vision and would have failed woefully. Don't be afraid of failure; believe in your vision and your God-given ability to fulfill them and you will surely succeed. Fear of failure will always stop you from trying and experimenting, thereby halting or quenching your thirst for innovation.

9. The **FEAR OF FALLING IN LOVE** is *"Philophobia".* This word originates from the Greek word *"filos"*, meaning loving, or beloved. Those who suffer from this fear are always afraid of romantic love, or forming emotional attachment. Such people have probably suffered heartbreak or disappointment in prior relationship. As a result, they are scared of falling in love again. This kind of fear mostly operates in women and that is why most women would not open their hearts to man in relationship again. Don't blame them; it is because of the fear of falling in love. Some who have managed to enter into relationships with this kind of fear don't really sacrifice their true love as far as the relationship is concerned and that is why they hardly give their all in the matters of love. The cure to the fear of falling in love is love itself, but not just the love in words, but perfect love borne out of God (1 John 4:18); ***"18 There is no fear in love; but perfect love casteth out fear: because fear hath torment. He that feareth is not made perfect in love."***

10. The **FEAR OF TRUSTING PEOPLE** is termed *"Pistanthrophobia."* This fear comes as a result of negative experiences either in a prior relationship or business venture. Though we live in a world where we don't really know who to trust, even the Bible attests to this truth (Micah 7:5); ***"5 Trust ye not in a friend, put ye not confidence in a guide: keep the doors of thy mouth from her that lieth in thy bosom."*** We live in a world where we can hardly trust pastors, business partners, friend, or family member, yet God does not want us to be entrapped in this bondage of fear. Many people have forfeited God-given opportunities due to

their fear of trusting people – the servant with one talent lost the opportunity of transacting his one talent to the expectation of his master because he did not trust his master. He said the master was an expert in reaping where he had not sown, this means he doesn't trust his master (Matthew 25:24): ***"24 Then he which had received the one talent came and said, Lord, I knew thee that thou art an hard man, reaping where thou hast not sown, and gathering where thou hast not strawed."*** Living in suspicion towards people is a bondage in itself – God wants us to be set free from such a bondage. Instead of being fearful in matters of trusting people, we should trust in God (Proverbs 3:5-6): ***"5 Trust in the LORD with all thine heart; and lean not unto thine own understanding. 6 In all thy ways acknowledge him, and he shall direct thy paths,"*** and He will always direct our paths to meeting the right people who deserve to be trusted. In as much as we are required not to be living in suspicion of friends, families, church members, business partners, and those who we come across on daily basis, there is a need for us to have guiding principles which should govern our lives so that we don't become vulnerable, and be victimized by the wicked, and the unreasonable people in this present world.

11. **FEAR OF DEMONIC ATTACK** in Greek is called *"Daemonophobia"*. It is an abnormal and persistent fear of evil. In Greek, "Daemon" means devil or evil spirit and *"phobos"* means fear. Those who are enslaved by this kind of fear become unduly anxious to seek for spiritual help. Consequently, they, out of ignorance, become victims in the hands of satanic agents.

    The devil can sometimes manifest evil images through your dreams expecting to see how you will react to what he has shown you. If your reaction is negative by exhibiting fear, he will establish a ground to use that method in manipulating you. You will consequently lose your peace, joy, and happiness. You will become so confused that you will seek for solution from satanic agents such as false prophets who disguise themselves as men of God. But if your reaction and response is positive by activating your faith, then you tap into the substance of the faith of God's Word in you which is your true identity, by so doing, you will experience peace, joy, happiness, and you will receive a divine direction for your life.

    Whatever you give your attention to will surely give you a direction. The devil will always attack your weak points. He will constantly hit that particular point of your life to gain your attention into worrying after fear has been established in your heart. One of the ways he does this is through nightmares. If you see nightmares in your dream and you brood over them mentally, it will develop into fear, and this fear will birth the reality of what you saw. Some people actually saw that they were sick, dead, and miserable in the dream and they chose to believe in that sSatanic lie rather than believing God's report. Any information that does not correspond to the will of God for your life is certainly from the devil. God's report is ultimately the true and final information for our lives, and we ought to hold on to that truth; if you mistakenly saw yourself miserable in your dream, that is not true. The devil is only throwing his darts at you to frighten you so as to gain an entrance into your life and reside there permanently.

Read these scriptures: 2 Corinthians 11:13-15; 2 Peter 2:1-3; Philippians 3:18-19.

There are many Christians, especially Africans, who are wallowing in ignorance and as a result become a channel of merchandizing and profitmaking for false prophets. They are deceived into believing that the cause of their problem is either demonic manipulation or witchcraft. The intention of false prophets is to establish the spirit of fear in the heart (mind) of their victims so that they can extort money from them. Such prophesy do not come to exhort, encourage or warn, but to keep their victims in the bondage of fear permanently.

They prophesy fearful lies to you to gain your attention to themselves. Prophecies do not come to make you panic or fear; any prophecy that does not encourage, warn you to living righteously, exhort and provide the right solution is not from God; it is from the devil. False prophets will leave you in a state of fear and confusion without the right solution. This could propel you to move from one prophet to the other in search of solution. This is a great frustration of the highest degree. God does not want you to live a frustrated life. Seek for the right knowledge, apply the knowledge in obedience to the principles of God's kingdom, be prayerful, and you will be free in Jesus name AMEN.

CHAPTER FIVE

THE ENTRANCE OF FEAR

How does fear enter our life? Though there is a spirit of fear in the world, it cannot have access into our lives unless we permit its entrance. In Job 3:25, Job said what he greatly feared had come upon him. Job was described as a perfect and upright man who feared God and hated evil in Job 1:1-3.

"1 There was a man in the land of Uz, whose name was Job; and that man was perfect and upright, and one that feared God, and eschewed evil. 2 And there were born unto him seven sons and three daughters. 3 His substance also was seven thousand sheep, and three thousand camels, and five hundred yoke of oxen, and five hundred she asses, and a very great household; so that this man was the greatest of all the men of the east."

But he failed to deal with the issues of fear regardless of his upright status before God – He allowed the spirit of fear to invade his mind and heart until what he was afraid of became a reality. No one knew Job's battle of fear until calamity befell him and that led to an open confession in Job 3:25; ***"25 For the thing which I greatly feared is come upon me, and that which I was afraid of is come unto me."*** It presupposes that Job had lived in the fear of losing his children, properties, riches, family, and servants. He also had the fear of being attacked with sickness; yet he was living a normal life like any other person. There are so many people battling with the agony of fear, and that has crippled their ability to make the right decisions and choices in life, but through the impartation of the Holy Spirit released through this Book, there shall be deliverance for your soul, spirit and body in Jesus name, Amen.

In Romans 10:17, we read, ***"17 So then faith cometh by hearing, and hearing by the word of God."*** In this verse, we clearly see how faith is generated to produce positive results. Faith comes through hearing of the Word of God; in the same way fear comes through words, but the words of Satan. Satanic words that generate fear come through voice and that is what I call the VOICE OF FEAR. The voice of fear surfaces in three dimensions:

THREE GATES OF FEAR

The voice of fear could be silent or loud:

1. Hearing
2. Seeing
3. Thinking

GATE OF HEARING

The voice of fear takes advantage of what we HEAR, SEE, and THINK TO CAPTURE OUR ATTENTION. About 95 percent of what we experience in life is borne out of what we HEAR, SEE, and THINK. This means that what we hear can either influence us negatively or positively. The Word of God is the VOICE OF GOD. That voice which passes through our sense of hearing is displayed in two ways: listening and reading – listening to and reading the Word of God; our sense of hearing is a vehicle through which God's Word is transported into our hearts.

"11 God hath spoken once; twice have I heard this; that power belongeth unto God" (Psalm 62:11).

When God speaks once, we are expected to hear twice – hearing through our physical sense of hearing and our heart. God does not speak to our flesh (mind), but he speaks to our spirits. Our heart is the seat of God's Spirit in us. For God to speak to our spirit, we must be born again. Though God speaks to everybody in diverse ways, He speaks clearly to His children through His Word (Jesus).

In Hebrews 1:1, we read that *"God, who at sundry times and in divers manners spake in time past unto the fathers by the prophets"* to their spirits. Our true identity is our spirit; the body is only a container that houses our real identity. In John 3:6, we learn that, *"That which is born of the flesh is flesh; and that which is born of the Spirit is spirit."* We became spirits the day our spirit became regenerated. God gave birth to us. It is the Spirit of God in us that gives us access to the voice of the Spirit of God in our hearts. This truth is reiterated in Romans 8:15-16: *"15 For ye have not received the spirit of bondage again to fear; but ye have received the Spirit of adoption, whereby we cry, Abba, Father. 16 The Spirit itself beareth witness with our spirit, that we are the children of God."* The spirit in us gives a technical knockout to the bondage of fear. When the Word of God enters our hearts, it transcends to the realms of our mind to constantly disengage it from all negative interactions that contradict the Word of God.

What we hear, see and think influence us positively or negatively as stated in Luke 21:9: ***"9 But when ye shall hear of wars and commotions, be not terrified: for these things must first come to pass; but the end is not by and by."*** What you hear becomes what you think about, and what you think about is what you see happen to you. Jesus is aware that the possibility to be afraid is terribly great if we HEAR certain information which areis terrifying. So, He warns us not to be terrified. God will not ask us to do what He has not empowered us to do. Do not be terrified. It means that even though fear could surface as a result of what we hear, God has given us the capacity to break its control over our lives. Your response to the terrifying reports or news you HEAR will determine the results you produce – Don't allow the negative news, economic crisis, doctors' and men's reports occupy your thoughts.

(1 Samuel 4:18*): "18 And it came to pass, when he made mention of the ark of God, that he fell from off the seat backward by the side of the gate, and his neck brake, and he died: for he was an old man, and heavy. And he had judged Israel forty years."* Prophet Eli failed to respond positively to the news he heard, fear took hold of him, broke his neck, and he eventually died. There are issues you will HEAR which might possibly trigger FEAR in you, but you ought to learn how to deal with your FEARS. The bad experiences that others face in life could become a voice that we HEAR, and that could lead to FEAR which can deny you the right to enjoy the promises of God.

(Numbers 13:32): ***"32 And they brought up an evil report of the land which they had searched unto the children of Israel, saying, The land, through which we have gone to search it, is a land that eateth up the inhabitants thereof; and all the people that we saw in it are men of a great stature."*** The Israelites began a journey over 40 years right from Egypt, and they had just few days (40 days) to enter the Promised Land, but the voice of evil report affected the morale of the people that they wept all through the night. Consequently, they murmured against God and the Promised Land eluded them. They lost peace, joy, and happiness as a result of the evil report.

Some people have few days to enter their marriage, breakthrough, success, or prosperity but a strange VOICE has denied them the opportunity to experience these promises. These are VOICES of fear. That voice of evil report, though sounded real, was false evidence but appeared real, but the VOICE contradicts the VOICE OF FAITH. Caleb and Joshua proved those reports wrong by exercising their FAITH based on the promise of God (Numbers 14:6-8): *"6 And Joshua the son of Nun, and Caleb the son of Jephunneh, which were of them that searched the land, rent their clothes: 7 And they spake unto all the company of the children of Israel, saying, The land, which we passed through to search it, is an exceeding good land. 8 If the LORD delight in us, then he will bring us into this land, and give it us; a land which floweth with milk and honey."*

GATE OF THINKING (MIND)

The human mind is the processor of thoughts. It is a realm of thoughts, imagination, and memory. God knows that our mind is the most sensitive part of the human make up. So it requires a constant renewal through the Word of God (Romans 12:2): *"2 And be not conformed to this world: but be ye transformed by the renewing of your mind, that ye may prove what is that good, and acceptable, and perfect, will of God."*

Our loin is what gives the strongest support to the entire body; otherwise the body will break down so God commanded us to guard the loins of our mind. Doubt is a mental state of mind to which indecision between belief and unbelief is displayed. This means that the mind is the key player in the issue of doubt. Doubt occurs in the realms of the mind. In Matthew 14:31, Jesus told us one of the reasons why Peter drowned. Jesus asked: why did you doubt? Fear took advantage of his thought to frustrate his movement from experiencing a great miracle

Satan is also aware that the mind of human beings is the most sensitive part of our frame. So he takes advantage of our mind (thinking pattern) to introduce fear. Most of the fearful things we imagine in the realms of our mind are not real;, they are simply false evidence appearing real in the realms of our minds. If fear is introduced through doubt produced by thought, and it is not effectively managed through the intervention of God's Word, the thought will grow to become a reality. If you keep pondering over negative things, they will definitely manifest. Whatever we experience, either negative or positive, is the product of our thoughts (Proverbs 23:7): *"7 For as he thinketh in his heart, so is he: Eat and drink, saith he to thee; but his heart is not with thee."* If you think continuously about failure, disappointment, poverty, shame, disgrace, death, etc., they have the capacity to manifest into reality if we fail to deal with them. Peter doubted and started sinking. His thought of doubt would have produced death if Jesus did not rescue him. May you be delivered from evil thought in Jesus name;. Amen.

SEEING GATE (SIGHT)

Anything you give your attention to will direct you. Walking by sight puts you in a state of disadvantage. For instance, if you are pursuing a particular course of action which you have actually invested your time, energy, and resources with an intention of becoming successful – and all of a sudden the devil opens up a fearful picture of another person who has already made the same or more effort than you have, yet he could not succeed, the possibility of being frustrated in the pursuit of your goal is great. (Mathew 14:29); *"29 And he said, Come. And when Peter was come down out of the ship, he walked on the water, to go to Jesus."* Jesus spoke the word of faith to Peter by saying "Come". Upon hearing the word he started walking upon the water – water sometimes in the Bible is referred to as trouble (Psalm 69:1); *"1 Save me, O God; for the waters are come in unto my soul."* (Isaiah 43:2); *"2 When thou passest through the waters, I will be with thee; and through the rivers, they shall not overflow thee: when thou walkest through the fire, thou shalt not be burned; neither shall the flame kindle upon thee."* He started walking upon his trouble, taking an advantage of the word of faith by walking on the trouble to meeting Jesus who represents Good News, breakthrough, and blessings. As you exercise your faith in the Word of God, I see you walking upon your trouble to the place of your blessing in Jesus name, Amen.

Whilst Peter walked upon the water to meet his blessing – he "saw" (SIGHT) the negative and fearful picture introduced to him through the devil which denied him access to arrive at the place of his blessing. (Numbers 13:28) *"28 Nevertheless the people be strong that dwell in the land, and the cities are walled, and very great: and moreover we saw the children of Anak there."* Instead of the spies to see God's unfailing promise that guarantees the possession of the land flowing with milk and honey, they saw the walls of impossibilities – they saw Children of Anaks (Giants). When their attention was focused on the impossibility to enter God's promise through the fear of seeing, they actually died in the wilderness without entering the Promised Land – this reminds of the first day I was sentenced to life imprisonment with hard labor – The devil showed me a horrible picture of myself where I quietly pictured myself so miserable, an old man with a stick so broken without any future again.

When I entered the prison yard, the walls were so tall and terrifying that one could easily resolve to committing suicide, but after surrendering my life to Jesus Christ, God helped me to overcome all my fears. And my sentenced was later committed to 30 years of which I have few years to complete. Glory be to God!

When you give your attention to negative pictures of any kind, you will end up becoming exactly what you see – Those who are always watching pornographic pictures will automatically become the same picture in the process of time. I declare that instead of focusing on your present situation of lack, poverty, sickness etc., you will rather look into the promises of God. (**Hebrews 12:2**) **"12:2 Looking unto Jesus the author and finisher of our faith; who for the joy that was set before him endured the cross, despising the shame, and is set down at the right hand of the throne of God"**. A policeman who met me in prison told me about how imprisonment has always been his fear. He said, anytime he drives and passes in front of the prison gate, the fear of prison will suddenly grasp him as soon as he sees, the gate. Thus, fear continues to torment him until the day when he walked in through the gate as a prisoner. You will always be entrapped by what you fear. (Proverbs 29:25): *"25 The fear of man bringeth a snare: but whoso putteth his trust in the LORD shall be safe."*

CHAPTER SIX

DANGERS OF LIVING IN FEAR

Knowing the consequences of certain negative decisions we make is enough to deter the wise from making such moves. God is wise and wants His children to operate in the higher dimension of wisdom; so that we can avoid all the dangers of life.

CONSEQUENCES

1. *(Job 1: 13 -19) "13 And there was a day when his sons and his daughters were eating and drinking wine in their eldest brother's house: 14 And there came a messenger unto Job, and said, The oxen were plowing, and the asses feeding beside them: 15 And the Sabeans fell upon them, and took them away; yea, they have slain the servants with the edge of the sword; and I only am escaped alone to tell thee. 16 While he was yet speaking, there came also another, and said, the fire of God is fallen from heaven, and hath burned up the sheep, and the servants, and consumed them; and I only am escaped alone to tell thee. 17 While he was yet speaking, there came also another, and said, The Chaldeans made out three bands, and fell upon the camels, and have carried them away, yea, and slain the servants with the edge of the sword; and I only am escaped alone to tell thee. 18 While he was yet speaking, there came also another, and said, Thy sons and thy daughters were eating and drinking wine in their eldest brother's house: 19 And, behold, there came a great wind from the wilderness, and smote the four corners of the house, and it fell upon the young men, and they are dead; and I only am escaped alone to tell thee"* (Job 1:13-19).

    "25 For the thing which I greatly feared is come upon me, and that which I was afraid of is come unto me" (Job 3:25).

    Fear breeds pain, sadness, sorrow and calamity. (Job 3: 25).

2. *"23 And he that doubteth is damned if he eat, because he eateth not of faith: for whatsoever is not of faith is sin"* (Romans 14:23).

    The opposite of faith is fear. Thus, fear breeds sin while faith breeds salvation. The just shall live by faith – anything done outside of faith sin before God. Faith leads to living in God while fear leads to sin, and sin leads to death.

3. *"25 And I was afraid, and went and hid thy talent in the earth: lo, there thou hast that is thine. 26 His lord answered and said unto him, Thou wicked and slothful servant, thou knewest that I reap where I sowed not, and gather where I have not strawed: 27 Thou oughtest therefore to have put my money to the exchangers, and then at my coming I should have received mine own with usury"* (Matthew 25:25-27). Fear denies us the opportunity to profit and make good success. One of the major reasons why the servant failed to experience profit is the spirit of fear: "For I feared." It also prevents us from using our spiritual gifts and talents.

4. *"71 And when he was gone out into the porch, another maid saw him, and said unto them that were there, This fellow was also with Jesus of Nazareth. 72 And again he denied with an oath, I do not know the man. 73 And after a while came unto him they that stood by, and said to Peter, Surely thou also art one of them; for thy speech bewrayeth thee. 74 Then began he to curse and to swear, saying, I know not the man. And immediately the cock crew"* (Matthew 26:71-74). Fear promotes lies, and it empowers the denial of Jesus Christ, and our faith in God.

5. *"8 But the fearful, and unbelieving, and the abominable, and murderers, and whoremongers, and sorcerers, and idolaters, and all liars, shall have their part in the lake which burneth with fire and brimstone: which is the second death"* (Revelation 21:8). Fear will deprive us of eternal life. The issue of fear is very serious and that is why it occupies the first position on the list of sins that stop us from making it to heaven.

6. *"30 Doubtless ye shall not come into the land, concerning which I sware to make you dwell therein, save Caleb the son of Jephunneh, and Joshua the son of Nun"* (Numbers 14:30). Fear denies us access to enjoying God's promises – it fear makes us see things in the natural, and not how God expects us to see them. Thus, we are compelled to run away because of fear; instead of having faith in the God who has promised and who will also fulfill His promises. He is a faithful God!

7. *"25 And I was afraid, and went and hid thy talent in the earth: lo, there thou hast that is thine"* (Matthew 25:25). Fear kills our ability to pursue our dreams, vision, and goals in life.

8. *"25 And I was afraid, and went and hid thy talent in the earth: lo, there thou hast that is thine"* (Matthew 25:25). Fear manipulates us into taking wrong decisions especially in marriage, business, and academics.

9. Fear causes a racing heart that leads to heart diseases and untimely death *"18 And it came to pass, when he made mention of the ark of God, that he fell from off the seat backward by the side of the gate, and his neck brake, and he died: for he was an old man, and heavy. And he had judged Israel forty years"* (1 Samuel 4:18).

CHAPTER SEVEN

FEAR NOT

"**10 Fear thou not; for I *am* with thee: be not dismayed; for I *am* thy God: I will strengthen thee; yea, I will help thee; yea, I will uphold thee with the right hand of my righteousness**" (Isaiah 41:10).

God knows the dangers of fear, and that is why He commanded us not to be AFRAID. God would not give us such a command if there was nothing wrong with being fearful. God is the commander of the whole universe, and whenever He gives a command, it is mandatory for us to obey Him.

"Fear not" is a command from God, not a suggestion. I have listened to several sermons on the subject of "fear not" and most preachers say, "'Fear not' is written in the Bible 365 times which means each day comes with its fear, but God has also made a provision of 'Fear not' for each day."

This statement sounds so encouraging, and it is absolutely true that God has already taken care of our fears for every second, minute, and hour. But after making diligent effort to search the scriptures, I realized that "fear not" does not appear 365 times in the Bible – I actually made this research for factual purposes, but that does not mean God's agenda for dealing with our daily fears is not guaranteed. "Fear not" is actually written 79 times in the Bible.

God created one big world, but within this world are several worlds created by men and circumstances. The world we see is not limited to the vast land mass. Every individual has the right to create his or her world within this world by the power of their choices. God did not create a world of poverty for anyone; men, by their own choices, have created the world of the poor, the rich, the great and small, educated and uneducated.

There are always two different kinds of people in the world, and every world has a particular language that is traceable to this world. Your world determines your language, and your language shows your identity. When those who identify with the world of poverty speak, you don't need a linguist to interpret their language; you just know where they belong; words like struggle continues, and words like, it's not easy ais are the   languages in the world of the lazy and poor. The kingdom of God's children identifies with the language of faith irrespective of their immediate conditions. In the world of the military, there is nothing like suggestion; they issue command. Glory be to God that we are also soldiers of Christ.

This is why Apostle Paul instructed us to put on the whole armor of God (Ephesians 6:11): ***"11 Put on the whole armor of God, that ye may be able to stand against the wiles of the devil."*** Those armoriesy are the arcutarmentaccouterment of the military. He was not suggesting to Christians but that statement connotes a command. The word of God says 'FEAR NOT.' This statement is from the commander-in-chief of the entire universe – He speaks and every other voice is silent. "Fear not" is not a suggestion, but a command in the Kingdom of God.

CHAPTER EIGHT

ANTIDOTES FOR FEAR

Psychologists have provided lots of techniques on how to deal with fear. But amazingly, all these techniques have failed. Some psychologists who seemed to have the antidote to fear ended up as victims which haves led some of them to suicidal death.

Fear is a spirit and combating it has nothing to do with exercising the physical body. It takes the preparedness of the mind for physical exercise to be properly carried out, but when fear comes, it does not only capture the heart but it disorganizes the mind from fulfilling its usual functions. Every spiritual situation needs a spiritual approach to yield positive results. How can I deal with my fear?

1. **YOU MUST BE BORN AGAIN**

   "4 For whatsoever is born of God overcometh the world: and this is the victory that overcometh the world, even our faith" (I John 5:4). You must be born again. Fear is of the world, and this world that I am talking about is the sSatanic world system – the world system is ruled and governed by Satan but the world of God says whosoever is born of God, in other words, whosoever is born again overcomes the world. It means that the first step to overcoming fear is to be BORN AGAIN. You need to escape from the world system to deal with your fears.. To be born again simply means to **REPENT**, To Repent means to turn from your sins and evil, and turn to God by believing that Jesus died, and was buried, and rose up on the third day for our justification, and confessing your sins to God, then you finally accept the Lordship of Jesus Christ in your life. Your victory to overcoming the spirit of fear is directly dependent on your faith in the Lord. until you are born again you still remain an enemy of God, and as long as you remain God's enemy you cannot overcome your fears. Worshipping God in an acceptable way requires faith in the Lord Jesus Christ, that's why when Jesus was addressing the issue of worship in the gospel of (John 4:24) He used the word **"MUST"**, in (Hebrews 11:6) the word **"MUST"** also appeared when the writer of

the book of Hebrew was dealing with the issue of faith in connection to worshipping God, in (John 3: 7) Jesus said unto Nicodemus, do not Marvel that I say you "**MUST**" be born again. All these references are pointing to the fact that the issue of being born is non-negotiable, it's a matter of **MUST**.

2. FOCUS AND BELIEVE IN GOD'S PROMISES

The word of God contains all the promises of God. And these promises are basically for His sons and daughters. The moment you doubt God's promises, you are denied access to experiencing what the word of God says concerning you.

"6 But let him ask in faith, nothing wavering. For he that wavereth is like a wave of the sea driven with the wind and tossed. 7 For let not that man think that he shall receive any thing of the Lord. 8 A double minded man is unstable in all his ways" (James 1:6-8). The word of God is so clear in this scripture that those who doubt God's promises cannot receive anything from Him. These people are unstable and double-minded in all their ways. To be double-minded refers to an individual who entertains two thoughts. If God says a double-minded man is blessed, healed, favored, protected, promoted, elevated, or secured, he/she entertains a contrary thought to what the word of God is saying. So, he cannot receive anything from the Lord. To be focused means HOLDING ON AND PERSISTING in one direction. It means that you have to believe God's word and hold on to that one thought. Not two thoughts but one. When you get one thought from God's word, and you get excited, then rumors, speculations, pains, insults and all manner of things come against you. These things come to suggest another thought to you.

There is a difference between joy and happiness. Happiness comes as a result of the good evidences around you; such as having money, getting married, and all sorts of pleasures you can think of. That is the limit to which happiness can go. The moment those things are no more in place, then worry, sadness, and sorrow becomes the order of the day. But joy is from the spirit of a Christian. It is one of the fruits of the Holy Spirit according to (Galatians 5:22). I have never seen a person operate in the realm of the joy of the Holy Ghost captured by fear or worry, because he or she is always joyful and rejoicing.

Apostle Paul was in prison; it was a terrible place but he constantly admonished the Church in Philippi to rejoice always. *"4 Rejoice in the Lord always: and again I say, Rejoice"* (Philippians 4:4). So, you can see that joy, or the spirit of joy, cannot be determined by the situation you find yourself. It goes beyond the physical evidences surrounding your life.

It is not about what happens to you but about what God is saying concerning that situation. It is important to note that you can't believe or focus on what you don't know; and that is why it is essential for every Christian to study God's word in-depth after being born again, so that you can continue to walk in God's promises.

3. **YOU MUST ALWAYS WALK BY FAITH**

5:7 (For we walk by faith, not by sight) (2 Corinthians 5:7). We become born again by grace through faith in Jesus Christ, and we are expected to continue to walk in the same faith in order to live a victorious life over the spirit of fear. *"4 For whatsoever is born of God overcometh the world: and this is the victory that overcometh the world, even our faith"* (1 John 5:4). Our ability to overcome the world of fear resides in the power of our faith in God. Your fear stops where your faith begins. Faith is believing in God without wavering. Our faith must be visible in action for God to see. Whiles our faith moves God, our fears moves Satan to accomplish his evil agenda in our lives. *"20 And when he saw their faith, he said unto him, Man, thy sins are forgiven thee."* (Luke 5:20). In this verse, we realize that it is possible for a multitude to be present in God's presence, and yet God will not notice their presence. Jesus did not see any human personality in the temple but their FAITH. Jesus did not say that He saw the sick man's four friends;, neither did he say he saw the church member or the congregant, but he saw their faith. It means that faith can be seen.

4. **YOU MUST ALWAYS RENEW YOUR MIND WITH THE WORD OF GOD**

"2 And be not conformed to this world: but be ye transformed by the renewing of your mind, that ye may prove what is that good, and acceptable, and perfect, will of God" (Romans 12:2). Our minds are the greatest battlefield where the devil pumps in so muchany false and wrong information. Whenever the mind receives an information, it communicates the message to the heart, and the heart releases it to the body to consummate it. Imagination is one of the functions of the mind; so any thought that contradicts the word of God should not be allowed to stay. (2 Corinthians 10:5)

"5 Casting down imaginations, and every high thing that exalteth itself against the knowledge of God, and bringing into captivity every thought to the obedience of Christ."

Renewal of our minds will exonerate us from conforming to the system of this world of which fear is inclusive. When you get born again, it is your spirit that got saved, not your mind. That is why it is still possible for you to assimilate certain unchristian thoughts. This is the more reason why our minds need constant renewal through God's word, so that we can always produce the right thoughts which will save us from being conformed to the pattern of this world.

5. **DECLARING THE WORD OF FAITH AGAINST YOUR FEARS**

"3 Though an host should encamp against me, my heart shall not fear: though war should rise against me, in this will I be confident" (Psalm 27:3). The word of God is spirit and life (John 6:63) and it is not only powerful but it is sharper and quicker than any two-edged sword of fear (Hebrews 4:12).

"12 For the word of God is quick, and powerful, and sharper than any two-edged sword, piercing even to the dividing asunder of soul and spirit, and of the joints and marrow, and is a discerner of the thoughts and intents of the heart." You can always rely on the word of God to deal with your fear. Though the word of God is powerful, it will yield no results until you declare what it says concerning your situation.

"17 I shall not die, but live, and declare the works of the LORD" (Psalm 118:17). In this psalm of David, He made a profound declaration and that declaration was born out of the situation that was confronting him at that particular moment when Saul was pursuing after him to kill him- Fear of death was so real in his life – but by divine understanding he has acquired through the knowledge of God's word – He quickly responded to the situation by declaring the word of faith against his fear. 'He says, I shall not die' but live to proclaim the goodness of God. Is there any situation that poses threat to your life?   Speak the word of God against it by faith, and you will see that situation succumb to the word of God in Jesus name Amen. – It's one thing to speak the word, and it's another thing to speak the word mixed with faith (Hebrew 4:2) words that are mixed with faith don't come out of our mind, they come out of our spirit with deep conviction, that those word works. Boxers who lost their fight actually lost before the fight

itself, they lost outside the boxing ring out of the fear of their opponents – I could remember in my primary school days, there was a certain boy who was always bullying me, engage me in a fight and beat me all the time. The reason I always lost the fight was because I had already accommodated defeat out of the fear of this particular boy. This intimidation continued until one day when I stopped being afraid of him, to my surprise, I beat him mercilessly after taking that decision – (Proverbs 29:25): *"25 The fear of man bringeth a snare: but whoso putteth his trust in the LORD shall be safe."* The snare of man entraps you. Anything you are afraid of becomes a trap against your life.

(1 Samuel 17:4): *"4 And there went out a champion out of the camp of the Philistines, named Goliath, of Gath, whose height was six cubits and a span."* Goliath decided to frighten the entire Israel with a taunting word and all of them went into hiding. The voice of fear denied them an opportunity to defeat their enemy. When David arrived at the scene, he also confronted the voice of fear with the voice of faith. He was not just speaking empty words, but his words have a strong source. He started mentioning the source of his faith from verse (1 Samuel 17: 45-47): *"45 Then said David to the Philistine, Thou comest to me with a sword, and with a spear, and with a shield: but I come to thee in the name of the LORD of hosts, the God of the armies of Israel, whom thou hast defied. 46 This day will the LORD deliver thee into mine hand; and I will smite thee, and take thine head from thee; and I will give the carcasses of the host of the Philistines this day unto the fowls of the air, and to the wild beasts of the earth; that all the earth may know that there is a God in Israel. 47 And all this assembly shall know that the LORD saveth not with sword and spear: for the battle is the LORD's, and he will give you into our hands."* This means his faith is produced from the word of (**THE LORD**) .David emphasized on the source of his strength and faith, it's no other person, than **THE LORD**. Goliath did not just scare and terrify the Israelites and King Saul. This fearful description of Goliath was so intimidating that anyone whose faith is not in the God of heaven cannot withstand him. Finally, he was described as a champion; this means he has never lost any fight before. Maybe there is a particular situation which has never missed target against their victims. If your faith is in place, you will defeat that situation (1 Samuel 17:4): *"4 And there went out a champion out of the camp of the Philistines, named Goliath, of Gath, whose height was six cubits and a span."*

From the verse 4-7 was all about the terrifying status and armory of Goliath but, those things did not move David because he was not operating by sight but by faith. In verse 8 Goliath asked a tricky question that every situation will demand from us, he says why have you come to battle with me? Fear will always give you the reasons you should surrender to its tricks.

The victory of David and the defeat of Goliath haves already been decided under the influence of the most powerful voice – The most powerful voice in this world is the voice of faith. Do not be afraid of that situation, have faith in God. Don't worry, the word of God is at your disposal, begin to speak it and you will see solutions without fail in Jesus Name Amen.

6. YOU MUST ALWAYS BE CONSCIOUS OF GOD'S PRESENCE WITH YOU

(Hebrews 13:5-6): *"5 Let your conversation be without covetousness; and be content with such things as ye have: for he hath said, I will never leave thee, nor forsake thee. 6 So that we may boldly say, The Lord is my helper, and I will not fear what man shall do unto me."* God is closer to us more than we can ever imagine. He is always with us in every ordeal situation that we find ourselves (Isaiah 43:1-2): *"1 But now thus saith the LORD that created thee, O Jacob, and he that formed thee, O Israel, Fear not: for I have redeemed thee, I have called thee by thy name; thou art mine. 2 When thou passest through the waters, I will be with thee; and through the rivers, they shall not overflow thee: when thou walkest through the fire, thou shalt not be burned; neither shall the flame kindle upon thee."* He did not redeem us to reject us. Many a times we run to men for help in our troubling moment and yet they fail us. Meanwhile God is just expecting us to be conscious of His presence with us and therefore, turn to Him for help.

Though fearful situation may rise up against us, but our God is bigger than all our fears (Psalm 23:4): *"4 Yea, though I walk through the valley of the shadow of death, I will fear no evil: for thou art with me; thy rod and thy staff they comfort me."* The secret of David is overcoming the spirit of fear that appeared to him in form of the valley of the shadow of death was the fact that he was conscious of God's presence in his life. He says because God is with him. Beloved you need to understand that God will not leave you nor forsake you, even in the deepest trouble and fear of your life – remember that God is always with you.

David was very sharp in the spirit, and he was aware that one of the strategies the devil uses to attack and manipulate his victim is the spirit of fear, so he addressed the situation from the basis of his consciousness of God's presence with him.

7. **TUNE YOUR HEART AND MIND TO THE HOLY SPIRIT** (Isaiah 30:21) *"21 And thine ears shall hear a word behind thee, saying, This is the way, walk ye in it, when ye turn to the right hand, and when ye turn to the left."* There are so many TV and Radio stations, but the choice to listen to or watch any station is at your disposal – Fear has got so many voices; Some through newspapers, economic crisis, evil reports, etc., but you should determine what kind of information you tune your heart and mind to listen to. Be led and connected to the antenna of heaven where bad news and negative information will not be broadcasted, and disconnect your mind and heart from fearful and negative news.

He shall not be afraid of evil tidings or evil news (Psalm 112:7,8); *"7 He shall not be afraid of evil tidings: his heart is fixed, trusting in the LORD. 8 His heart is established, he shall not be afraid, until he see his desire upon his enemies.""*, in order words he shall not be afraid of Satanic lies, because his heart is stayed on the Lord that means his heart is established meaning his heart is cemented on God's word and nothing from the pit of hell can penetrate it. David said that Lord has established his feet upon the rock;, rock is very solid that not even bullets can penetrate. That rock is Jesus Christ. If your life is established on the word which is Jesus Christ, no fiery darts of the devil can penetrate your life – Hallelujah!!!

Fear, then, is the result of lack of faith, not believing in God's power and especially His love and willingness to act on our behalf. The fearful are that way because they lack faith. Jesus Christ reveals this connection in (Mark 4:40): *"40 And he said unto them, why are ye so fearful? hHow is it that ye have no faith?"* But he said to them, why are you so fearful? How is it that you have no faith? When Jesus Christ saw fear, His immediate response was to question that person's faith. Fear is a very human reaction. As Christ indicates how we respond depends on our degree of faith – When faith is weak or non-existent, fear becomes the controlling factor rather than faith. We begin to live by sight and not by faith (2 Corinthians 5:7): *5:7 (For we walk by faith, not by sight) :* and without faith in Christ Jesus, no one can be saved. We are saved by grace through faith in Christ Jesus. And to who did He swear that they would not enter into His rest but to those who did not obey? So we see that they could not enter in because of unbelief (Hebrews 3:18-19): *"18 And to whom sware he that they should not enter into his rest, but to them that believed not? 19 So we see that they could not enter in because of unbelief".*

We see in the case of Peter walking on water that doubt causes fear, but we also saw a hint on how we can combat that fear and get it under control. As long as Peter kept his focus on Christ, he could do the impossible but once he began walking by sight, fear gripped him under its control, and he was no longer able to do the impossible. Even though fear is a natural and specific human emotion, do we control it or does it control us?

The devil has not changed from being a liar! Whenever the devil lies to you, and you keep on imagining his lies, then his lies will gradually be forming in your mind until it becomes a reality of what he has said to you which is completely opposite to what God is saying or has said about you. The devil has never spoken the truth about you to yourself before and don't expect him to start saying the truth about you. He will always paint a sad and evil picture about yourself to you (James 1:23-25): *"23 For if any be a hearer of the word, and not a doer, he is like unto a man beholding his natural face in a glass: 24 For he beholdeth himself, and goeth his way, and straightway forgetteth what manner of man he was. 25 But whoso looketh into the perfect law of liberty, and continueth therein, he being not a forgetful hearer, but a doer of the work, this man shall be blessed in his deed."* That is why you need to constantly look unto the mirror of the word of God where you can clearly see your image as a blessed child of God and not those lies.

8. PPRAISING AND PRAYING: Praising and praying in the midst of a terrifying situation is one of the antidotes to dealing with the spirit of fear. David wrote (75) psalms, psalms means: a sacred song used in praising and worshiping God. remember that the life of David was full of battles, fears from his son Absalom, fears from Ahithophel his counselor and friend, fears from king Saul, fear from the philistines and the Amalekites, but in all these David was busy getting addicted to praising God. No wonder he was honored by God by calling him a man after His heart. When your heart is full of God's praise, your life shall be free from satanic fears. Paul and Silas were arrested and were sent into a very deadly prison, they applied one of the antidotes which cannot fail whenever fear surfaces, they saw the bigness of God more than the terrific situation they were confronted with, instead of being afraid, they began to praise God, the

foundation of the prison began to shake, and the gates of the prison got opened without struggle . Praising God in the midst of your fear is a great weapon and antidote that does not miss target. (2 chronicles 20:1-3) Jehoshaphat was confronted with an issue that was so terrible, three nations were coming to attack Judah, Judah means praise, the fear was directed against their praise to God, he was engulf with the spirit of fear, but after inquiring from the Lord, he received a divine secret that cannot fail no matter the gravity of your fear. He was directed by God to sing praises to Him, and deliverance from fear was established, the enemies that came to fight them started helping each other to destroy themselves. Begin to praise God and you will see that mountain of fear standing before you crumble permanently in Jesus name; Amen. Let me share the story of the couple who wrote this song: "Because He Lives" is the song I am referencing, of course. The Gaithers' story began in the community of Alexandria, Ind., where Bill and Gloria met while teaching high school together. Bill had roots in Southern Gospel music and began the Bill Gaither Trio (joined by his brother Danny and his sister Mary Ann) while he was a student at Anderson College (now Anderson University), a Christian college in Anderson, Ind. Soon after Bill and Gloria met, they began to share ideas about songs. Gloria had been an English major in college so she had a strong command of language and vocabulary. Not long after they were married (in 1962), Gloria took Mary Ann's place in the trio and, by 1967, Bill was devoting his full-time attention to their career in music.

But the 1960s were a chaotic era and the quantum shift in values was deeply disturbing to Bill and Gloria. They had begun to wonder if God hadn't given up on the world. The winter of 1969 was a particularly bleak one for them. Not only had the Indiana winter been a long and hard one, with the north wind blowing even more fierce than usual for that region, Bill had been stricken with a severe case of mononucleosis. At the same time, Gloria and some other members of their church family encountered some painful false accusations and belittlement. As you can imagine, this was a very hard time for both Bill and Gloria.

She remembers sitting in their living room in agony and fear on New Year's Eve. Across the nation, the educational system was being infiltrated with the "God is dead" idea, while drug abuse and racial tension were increasing. The older generation felt that the country's best days were behind them and their baby boomer children agreed (yet, both felt that the others were to blame). Sound familiar? It was about this time that Bill and Gloria discovered that they had a baby on the way. It was wonderful news, yet it also concerned them. Was it really a wise thing to bring a baby into such a world? One sunny day in the early spring, Bill, Gloria and Bill's father George walked across the paved parking lot at their small A-frame offices. George called Bill and Gloria's attention to a spot they had not noticed. He pointed out a tiny blade of grass that had pushed aside layers of dirt, rock and concrete to reach the sunshine of the world above. It had such a strong will to live; it had overcome all the odds to fulfill its destiny. That blade of grass became a symbol to the Gaithers of how God works in His creation. And it inspired Gloria to write a song expressing the hope that was shaped by the resurrection of Jesus, as well as that blade of grass and the birth of her son.

"God sent His Son, they called Him Jesus; He came to love, heal and forgive. He lived and died to buy my pardon; An empty grave is there to prove my Savior lives. ... How sweet to hold a newborn baby; and feel the pride and joy he gives; but greater still, the calm assurance: This child can face uncertain days because He lives. ... Because He lives, I can face tomorrow. Because He lives, all fear is gone. Because I know He holds the future, and life is worth the living just because He lives!"

CHAPTER NINE

THE POWER OF WORDS

The word we speak, hear and listen to are moving under the influence of the spirit, and they will always produce two different results; life or death. Every word we speak is spirit, GOOD WORD - GOOD RESULTS = LIFE. EVIL WORDS – EVIL RESULTS = DEATH. It produces result even though we don't see those words as they are proceeding out of our mouths and that is why they are spirits. Just as the wind blows and nobody knows where it is coming from and where it is going to (John 3:8), but we feel and see its effects, so are the words we speak, hear and listen to.

The words we speak are spirits and life. Our hearts are the seat of the Spirit where words are being produced (Matthew 12:34-37); *"34 O generation of vipers, how can ye, being evil, speak good things? for out of the abundance of the heart the mouth speaketh. 35 A good man out of the good treasure of the heart bringeth forth good things: and an evil man out of the evil treasure bringeth forth evil things. 36 But I say unto you, That every idle word that men shall speak, they shall give account thereof in the day of judgment. 37 For by thy words thou shalt be justified, and by thy words thou shalt be condemned."* Out of the abundance of the heart, the mouth speaks. That is why we believe God's word with our hearts and not with our minds. The mind functions in three dimensions, namely: Memory, Imagination (thought), and Meditation. That is why Satan takes advantage of its functions to manipulate our thought processes. When you get born again, your spirit is saved and the devil cannot stay there with the Holy Spirit and Jesus in the same house, but he can manipulate your mind, if you don't engage it in constant renewal through God's word, but Satan can stay in an unregenerated heart, and that is the one who has not been saved. Anytime the devil wants to carry out his evil agenda, he uses any form of vessels, especially human beings.

The mind is a battlefield where the devil throws so many darts. That is why by the inspiration of the Holy Spirit, Apostle Peter admonishes the Christians to guard the loins of their mind (1 Peter 1:13): ***"13 Wherefore gird up the loins of your mind, be sober, and hope to the end for the grace that is to be brought unto you at the revelation of Jesus Christ;""*** – refuse negative information to stay in there. You can allow a bird to fly over your head but you cannot allow it to make a nest on your head. If that information remains in your mind, you will begin to believe them, and you will end up confessing them and that would lead you to believing them. Consequently, you become the exact picture of the information on your mind, which is contrary to God's intention for your life.

(Revelation 12:11); ***"11 And they overcame him by the blood of the Lamb, and by the word of their testimony; and they loved not their lives unto the death."*** There are two kinds of weapons that guarantee our victory over the works of the enemy:. The blood of Jesus, and the world of our testimony. There is God's responsibility and the Christian's responsibility in activating these weapons. God's responsibility in this deal is to offer the blood of His only begotten Son, Jesus Christ, and that has been done and established already. The Christian's responsibility is to enforce our words of testimony over Satan and his schemes by faith. Those testimonies are good reports, good news, and not false reports of the devil. This is why the Christian is not permitted to speak failure or negativity. The word coming into our hearts is spirit and life by the vehicle of faith. So, life is expected to proceed out of our mouth, despite the negative evidences surrounding your life.

In Genesis 1:1-3, tThere was a chaotic and formless evidence whilst God was creating the earth, but He did not confess based upon those obvious evidences. He rather spoke light and life into the situation and the situation responded to correction immediately, because the word carries power to create, influence and change every situation to our advantage. The choice to speak the right word that produces the right result is at our disposal. Your victory or defeat will be determined by the choice of words we speak. The word of our testimony is exclusively important that it has to be tied to the blood of Jesus in order to establish our victory. Though we believe with our hearts, but believing without confessing will produce no positive result, even though our victory is already declared by God. (2 Corinthians 4:13): ***"13 We having the same spirit of faith, according as it is written, I believed, and therefore have I spoken; we also believe, and therefore speak."*** We believe; therefore, we speak!!! All the wars and battles we have ever experienced were influenced by certain negative words that produced death. The word of Jezebel (the wife of Ahab) against

Elijah, did not die, because those words are spirits and spirits don't die. She issued a threat against the Prophet that his head will be cut off and this word continued to live until the arrival of John the Baptist (interestingly it was a woman that ordered the beheading of the second, who is John the Baptist), who came in the spirit and power of Elijah. This incident would have been averted, if Elijah had confronted that evil declaration with the word of faith, but instead he ran away simply because he was afraid.

(Malachi 4:5-6); Prophet Malachi prophesied that Elijah will come before the coming of the great and dreadful day of the Lord. This prophecy came to pass before the eyes of the disciples and the people that were around Jesus Christ in that dispensation. Jesus was aware that this theology will be too difficult for people to understand so he concluded by saying, 'if you can accept it'; meaning he does not want to force this truth upon anybody. Read these scriptures for clarification: Malachi 4:5-6; Luke 1:13-17, Mark 6:14-24, Matthew 11:13-15.

You have to get rid of the old information and the lies of the devil off your mind, and replace them with the right knowledge (information) in God's word. There are people who take delight in keeping memories of regrets, disappointments, fears, failure and hurts. You realize that those bad memories come to play frequently and that creates unhappy mood for you. Therefore, you confess negative words and you get negative results in return. Renew your mind with good news (the good testimonies of what God is doing what he has done in your life). No matter how bad you think your condition is, it is still not the worst. That condition is still far better than millions of people out there. There are many people who wish to be in your condition, yet they don't have such opportunity. I also wish to be free from this prison right now, even though I am in prison, my condition is still far better than many people out there simply because I have Jesus Christ living in me.

James 3: 2-6 say *"2 For in many things we offend all. If any man offends not in word, the same is a perfect man, and able also to bridle the whole body. 3 Behold, we put bits in the horses' mouths, that they may obey us; and we turn about their whole body. 4 Behold also the ships, which though they be so great, and are driven of fierce winds, yet are they turned about with a very small helm, whithersoever the governor listeth. 5 Even so the tongue is a little member, and boasteth great things. Behold, how great a matter a little fire kindleth! 6 And the tongue is a fire, a world*

of iniquity: so is the tongue among our members, that it defileth the whole body, and setteth on fire the course of nature; and it is set on fire of hell." Positive words can reframe your life and make it more meaningful, but negative words can kindle fire of confusion, divorce, fighting, and etcetera. All these mentioned are the products of negative words spoken by certain people who lacked the understanding of the mystery of the word. Speak the right word and get the right results. God bless you, Amen.

www.ingramcontent.com/pod-product-compliance
Lightning Source LLC
Chambersburg PA
CBHW050507120526
44588CB00044B/1723